Life in Tune

LIFE

IN

TUNE

Personal Transformation
Through Music and
Mindful Mastery

Barry A. Lehman

Contents

local municipal band directed by a member of the church I was serving who was soon to become my best friend. I joined and loved the wonder of playing again. Practice was minimal and, since the band was mainly a summer-in-the-park band, I tended to add the practice for that to the Christmas and Easter opportunities. We did have a trombone choir at the church and I purchased a soprano trombone (or is it a slide trumpet?) which got me more practice times.

My practice, overall, was sporadic, but not nonexistent. I got myself a new (used) trumpet- a Bach Strad and found I could play better than I thought. I started doing music with campers at our church camps. I attended a jazz camp at UW-Whitewater for my 50th birthday. (I was the only adult student there.) From then until moving to Rochester, Minnesota in 2010 I continued the same general practice schedule and involvement, when possible, in a community band and church. Rochester has a wealth of musical opportunities. Within two years I was playing in a community band and a big band. Soon there would be a brass quintet, another community band, and another big band. The big bands pushed me more than the community bands did. I knew how to play the traditional band language; the jazz language was mainly in my head and had not translated into the horn. I took some lessons from a local trumpet player/ teacher. I practiced more regularly. I even went back and pulled out the good, old Arban's book. I was excited.

In June 2015 I went to a Shell Lake Arts Center adult workshop on big bands. I was inspired and motivated. As part of the workshop, we had a Master Class for the trumpets. Bob Baca, the leader, did one small thing on playing trumpet. I was blown away. My playing changed almost immediately.

That's the musical beginning of what has become this book.

The first week of August 2015, spurred by one of the other big band trumpet players and Mr. Baca, I went back to Shell Lake for the Trumpet Workshop. Unlike the Big Band weekend, this was for all ages, although most were high school and first year college students. This was even more exciting and motivating, led also by Bob Baca and a faculty of diverse trumpet players. They were a class act that saw trumpet playing as more than just the techniques, but included the motivational, psychological, and social insights about success.

Again, I was challenged... and blown away. This time my embouchure (lip) was in better shape and I was able to play longer and in better tone than in June.

I also discovered again the real joy of being in a place where music ruled. One of the other "adult" students commented that it was great to be around a large group of "trumpet nerds."

The faculty gave us lessons, challenges, and opportunities to play. The showed us how to practice and shared their many stories and experiences with us. On the last morning we all sat in the rehearsal hall and were asked to share what we remembered from the week. Since most of us only remember things for about three days without reinforcement, this was an important part of the "taking it home" process. Most of what was remembered were the ideas and thoughts that motivated us.

As I took notes I thought, "This would make a great blog series!" Next, I decided that it needed more than just my usual *Wanderings of a PostModern Pilgrim* blog. It needed a blog of its own, even if I would cross-post on both. Since much of what we learned and experienced is more than applicable to the ways we live each day I knew that it would also be a reflection on how music and our experiences at the workshop made a difference in the rest of the year. So why not do a weekly post that keeps the ideas and motivation going for the 48 weeks left until the next camp?

Which brings me to the original title of the blog: *The Tuning Slide.* On a trumpet, the tuning slide is the curved "C"-shaped tube at the opposite end of the lead pipe from the mouthpiece. The slide is to be used to bring the trumpet into tune with the other instruments.

When you are in tune

- The music flows much more smoothly.
- You tend to get into sync with the other musicians.
- You don't get as tired while playing since you are not constantly trying to "lip" the notes into tune.

In short, the tuning slide keeps us moving more smoothly in the right direction. That is what I hope comes from this blog and these blog posts- ways that even non-trumpet players and non-musicians can discover how to keep life more "in tune."

As I started the blog posts, I asked my readers to join with me and the faculty and students from the trumpet camp of August 2015 on this journey. I felt that there were some neat things to share and hopefully they would find themselves getting in- and staying in tune with themselves and others around them.

A year passed. There were more than forty posts. I decided to collect them into a single "book" with little to no revision. I changed the order so some would be together with other posts of the same topic. I did some changing of words to fit a collection rather than a weekly blog post. Bob Baca and I decided to make the book available at no cost to the students in the 2016 Shell Lake Trumpet Camp which I accomplished through a Go Fund Me campaign.

That is the first section of this book- The First Year.

I then continued the blog, taking notes again, picking up on old ideas with new insights. I kept finding ever new ways to talk about the connections between being a musician and of living life. The faculty of Shell Lake Trumpet Workshop continued to be available and far more than just helpful. They became mentors and guides in what I was doing. Comments and questions from other students would spur me to examine something new. Trumpet colleagues kept giving me directions to go. The journey continued.

At the heart of it was my ongoing trumpet playing. In my "retirement" I had the time to practice nine days out of ten and anywhere from sixty to ninety minutes a day. I still played in the musical ensembles I mentioned earlier- big bands, concert bands, and brass quintet. I have taken small steps into improvisation as one who has loved jazz for well over 50 years. I have been having fun while learning and growing.

As I came to the end of the second year of the blog, I decided to republish the series covering two years of writing, learning, and playing. I kept the two years as separate sections- year two is the second section of the book. I hope that the sense of movement and growth will be more obvious by keeping year two in its chronological place.

I then continued on with the blog for another 2 years. I circled around on subjects, developed new insights, deep some deeper diving into some things and found new ideas I had never known before. I began year five in August 2019. I started with a "letter" to Mr. Baca, summarizing where the four years had taken me, noting the repeating and growing themes. Who knew that the world was about to shift under all our lives?

In March 2020 I wrote one more post about music in a time of pandemic. As it turns out I had no idea what we were all about to face. That was the last post in the blog. I stopped writing it, holed up in my "safer at home" world and tried to figure out what was happening next. I ended up completely retiring from my counseling position and started wrestling with the "What next?" question. It turned into a new career as a full-time author. As far as music was concerned, there were no gigs to do, no rehearsals (other than some brave attempts at it) and I kept on practicing. Mostly.

It is now one year after the start of the pandemic. As I pivoted into my new career, I decided to do another edition of this book. Some friends and colleagues told me in a lot of nice ways that the original title didn't quite make it. Most people, they said, would never get to the subtitle about life and music. With the help of the incredible people at Self-Publishing School and a course with Amazon Ad School I decided to do a new edition with a new title. The first two sections remain the same. But I have discovered some new things as a result of trying to play music in a pandemic and keep my skills up. So, I have added a new postlude on staying "in tune" during a global pandemic and crisis. There will be more information in that postlude bringing you up to date on what I have done and learned. In some ways it will bring together in several posts the way music, mastery, and mindfulness have kept me going and changing in all of this.

Hence the new title, describing my journey since that first camp in 2015, makes more sense than I would have thought possible way back then.

Journey with me then into living Life in Tune!

Notes:

- Internet links indicated in the book were all live at the time of this writing. I have tried to remove any that were lost over the years. My apologies for any that were missed.
- I mention a number of exercise, study, and etude books. These are the essentials in the trumpet repertoire. I refer to them simply by name in the text. Arban, Charlier, Clarke, Concone, Getchell, and Schlossberg. There are many others, of course, but these are the standards.

There are many music people who have helped make this book possible over the past fifty-plus years:

- *Junior and Senior High band directors:* Leo Caprio, Frank Schoendorfer, and Lawrence Cooper.
- *Director of "Tijuana Brass" and Church Brass group:* Harold Fravel
- *College Band Directors:* Jonathan Elkus, Albertus Meyers
- *Community Bands and Orchestras Directors:* Tom Heninger, Barry Fox, Rich Batchelor, Mike Mangan, Chuck Blattner, Brock Besse, Tony Boldt, Jonathan Knutson, Joe Riemer, Roger Jones, Jason Rinehart.
- *Trombone Choirs Directors:* Jeff Reynolds and Lois Mease.
- *Church Praise Band director:* Cody Johnson
- *Trumpet Mentors and Friends:* Warren Bandel, Steve Bingner, Jeff Mason, Ron Post, Janet Olson, Mark Bergquist, Brian Sander, Ellis Workman.
- *Shell Lake Trumpet Faculty* (who have also become friends): Bill Bergren, Matt Mealy, Kyle Newmaster, John Raymond, Matt Stock, Paul Stodolka
- *My Guru:* Bob Baca

Dedicated in memory of Leah Allert.

She introduced me to the Rochester Big Band and helped open a whole new chapter of my life. She is gone too soon.

Year One

Crazy Good- Getting Started

Just because something seems "crazy" doesn't mean it's bad. Or worse- impossible. In the first year I found that it's not crazy for a semi-retired 67-year-old to decide to become a "full-time" musician. Even after over 50 years of playing at various levels, there's always more. It sounds crazy but as I learned at the first Shell Lake Trumpet Workshop in 2015, when someone says:

That's crazy, man.

The answer is

Yeah. Crazy good!

Chapter 1.1

The Mind of a Child

The greatest invention in the world is the mind of a child.

-Thomas Edison

Watch a child discover something new. They will explore every bit of it. They will turn it over, touch it, play with it, even put it in their mouth if we let them. Watch a child watching and you will see wonder expressed. Watch a child thinking and you will see wheels turning that we have long forgotten in our rush to adulthood. Life is always challenging, wonderful, strange, new, scary, hopeful, eternal.

Watch a musician learning a new song, attacking a difficult passage, playing a solo and nailing it. You will often see that same wonder being expressed. That sound, that passage, that solo has never been played like that before- and the musician knows it. To come to the music- and life in that way allows for the possibilities and surprises that result in awe and joy.

Just like kids.

I posed the question of having the mind of a child to the group from the Trumpet Workshop.

Brandyn described it to me:

> Kids don't think- they just do. When I play and sound my best I'm not thinking about anything except the music. I literally just sing it in my head at times and it's amazing. Just gotta keep the mind of a child and go for the music!

Cody said:

> that when "Having the Mind of a Child" you don't let your ego interfere with the learning process. For example, in "The Inner Game of Tennis", Timothy Gallwey uses the example of when a child learns to walk. When they fall, they don't get down on themselves.

It's a shame that we lose the mind of a child when we grow up. Not that we should continue to be immature or illogical, but that we should be ready and willing to let the creative juices of childhood flow. We should be ready and willing to kick back and let the moment happen.

Sometimes the best answer is the simplest that doesn't take a lot of complex interpretations. Sometimes it is just letting our lives become the lives they already are and not worry about what that might look like.

It is in the trying that we achieve our first successes and not judging the goodness or badness of what we have done. Like Cody said- keep the ego out of it. It works when learning to play music. It works when learning to live life.

If it works, why stop?

Chapter 1.2

About Trumpets

"Ah, the trumpet. Now there's an instrument on which one can truly embarrass himself!"

(G. Keillor to G. Bordner)

A trumpet is a musical instrument. It has the highest register in the brass family. As a signaling device, trumpets have a very long history, dating back to at least 1500 BC; they have been used as musical instruments since the 15th century. They are played by blowing air through almost-closed lips, producing a "buzzing" sound that starts a standing wave vibration in the air column inside the instrument. Since the late 15th century, they have primarily been constructed of brass tubing, usually bent twice into a rounded oblong shape.

-Wikipedia

What is so special about the trumpet?

First- it is often the lead, giving the melody a good ride, soaring over the other instruments. Yet, it is not the only lead. Others can and do take the lead parts that give new insight and direction to the music.

Second- it is easily learned, but is deceptive in its difficulties. To maintain one's skill at trumpet, one must be willing to work, regularly. Too much time off and you notice the problem. Again, other instruments are in the same boat, but because the trumpet stands out so easily and carries so far it can be downright embarrassing when you are not at your best.

I was sold on the trumpet with three individuals who I will no doubt talk about more over the months. I am not even sure any more who I heard first. The three settled my mind on the trumpet and no one could keep me from it. Louis Armstrong, Al Hirt, and Herb Alpert set me on this road. *When the Saints Go Marching In, Java, and The Lonely Bull/Tijuana Taxi* were the songs that allowed the trumpet to shine.

Many others have come along and had a great influence, but these three set the tone for me. But I also learned that the trumpet has a great part in classical music as much as it does in jazz. Sousa marches are another dimension.

Some might say that the trumpet is only interesting to those who like to stand out, be obvious, overpower others. While there may be a (very, very) small kernel of truth in that, the place of the trumpet allowed me to express myself in ways that my uncertain shyness never allowed me to. What a joy.

Of course, the trumpet isn't the only instrument in the world that can do this, in spite of what most trumpet players might have you believe. For me, with the trumpet, depending on the part you are playing, the trumpet can have all kinds of different ways to express itself- the lead in first trumpet, a nice count-er-melody in third, wonderful harmony in second, sometimes doubling the passage with other instruments, sometimes being there on your own.

Sadly, in many bands, even community bands, it is often the practice to use the stronger trumpets on first and the weakest on third. This can happen because, naturally, the weaker ones cannot play the first parts. But I have found that a section of trumpets where all can play any of the parts, makes for a strong sound from the trumpets. Plus, having accomplished players playing with the weaker ones on 2nd or 3rd, helps the weaker ones grow and develop.

There are no secondary or inferior parts. We only make them that way by our attitude. As the great trumpeter and composer W. C. Handy said in the quote at the top of this post- that's a lot like life itself. The trumpet does not play itself. One does not become proficient at anything, including trumpet, without putting work into it.

Nor does it mean that because one does not have all the incredible talents of the "stars" that one is inferior as a human being. I will never be Louis Armstrong or Maynard Ferguson, but I can be the best I can be. In my life, as an old Jewish story goes, God will not ask me why I wasn't Moses or Abraham or any other great and talented individual. God will just ask me why I didn't do the best I could with what I have and who I am.

Chapter 1.3

Wow! or Not: A Musician's Mind

Music is the shorthand of emotion.

— Leo Tolstoy

Like most of us I have been "Wowed!" by a performance, event, situation. I will sit there with mouth agape wondering how in the world they did that?

In doing some surfing on the Internet I discovered that there is a whole understanding of "Wow!" as something to aim for. Two headers on a Google search said:

- Good Customer Service is Over -- WOW Your Customers
- Ways To Stop Satisfying Customers And Start Wowing Them

I even found a book for choral musicians

- The Wow Factor: How to Create It, Inspire It & Achieve It: A Comprehensive Guide for Performers by Steve Zegree

The Urban Dictionary defines the "wow factor":

- A set of properties belonging to an object that pleasantly surprise a watcher. (www.urbandictionary.com/)

And the Cambridge dictionary says:

- a quality or feature of something that makes people feel great excitement or admiration. (dictionary.cambridge.org/us/dictionary/english/)

Pleasant surprise, excitement and admiration. Yep.

As a musician such a moment can be inspirational to me- or send me to give up on even trying. My favorite joke when listening to such a trumpet performance is simply, "They didn't put those notes into my trumpet."

Which of course isn't true.

But being "Wowed!" by a performance may actually work against us as musicians. It can get in the way of experiencing the music on a deeper level. When we feel "Wow!" we move away from the music itself and fall into our emotional response. Not a bad thing, of course, as I will talk about in a little bit, but at that moment we end up becoming lost in our response and ignoring what is happening in the music itself that is making us feel this way.

I don't mean that we should sit in detached disinterest and listen to the music as if it were some class assignment. Nor do I mean that we should sit and analyze every moment of music that we hear to see what it is doing.

Rather I see the need to catch the "Wow!" and let it be real, not an overwhelming of our emotions by the music, but having the music flow through us in a way that we can feel and touch its meanings and movements.

The emotional response I mentioned is not something to be avoided or to fall 150% into. Rather it is a cue- a trigger- that says to me, when it happens, that there is something exciting and important happening here in this music. It is moving me; it is making my inner self sit up and pay attention; it is grabbing hold of me.

- What is happening?
- What's going on here?
- Why is it touching me in this way?

Another word to describe this is one I feel is an essential to daily life: Mindfulness.

When the "Wow!" happens, it is calling me to mindfulness. It is calling me to pay attention to what is happening in my life at this very moment through this music.

I remember a Wynton Marsalis concert I attended 25 years or so ago. I no longer remember the piece he played, but I remember a moment when he finished off a solo in the most incredibly moving way. As it ended and I exhaled with a quiet "Huh!" I heard someone else in the audience do the same thing just before the applause started. I figured it was another trumpet player who understood the feeling of that solo.

I didn't analyze it, I let it happen and gave thanks for the moment. It was not a "Wow!" as much as it was a moment of awareness. I felt myself as real IN the moment as Wynton's notes touched me. When we get stuck in the "Wow!" we can lose that mindful awareness.

To grow as a musician, I need to listen to the kind of performances that might contain the "Wow!" but I cannot be overcome by them. I have to learn to live in them and them to live in me. I can then learn to find that same mindfulness as I play my music. It's just being present. And experiencing it.

Which is what mindfulness as daily life is all about. When we are willing to be open to what is going on around us and acknowledge its power, we are not being "Wowed!" We are rather, living in the possibilities of the moment.

Chapter 1.4

Watching with Wow! and Insight

I talked about the "Wow!" factor in the previous section and how it is important not to fall prey to it in the sense of being overwhelmed and not getting intimidated by the music (or other things.) Well, then I came across a trumpet quintet video that blew me away. My first reaction was "Wow!" But as I kept watching I allowed the music to move me and my understanding to flow from it.

The article was headlined *Oklahoma State University win the Getzen Trumpet Small Trumpet Ensemble Division with "Toccata and Fugue in D minor (Bach)" at the 2015 National Trumpet Competition.* It was as excellent example of Wow! And what to watch for when you begin to feel it. The video has been viewed over 1.5 million times in five years! Even if you don't watch it, pay attention to my thoughts below about what makes for a Wow! performance.

(If you want to watch the performance on YouTube: https://www.youtube.com/watch?v=YNLv2exFwqc)

My first thoughts- any brass group doing a decent job on a Bach transcription deserves the "Wow!" The music of J S Bach is always spectacular and moving. Bach touches so many sides of the human experience that one must allow the music to live on its own. Math and magic and amazingly well-constructed phrases make Bach untouchable. His "Toccata and Fugue" ranks among his greatest works. The toccata shows the "improvisational" touch and the fugue the polyphonic structures. Originally written for organ, a brass transcription has to take certain liberties. Any group wanting to perform it has to know the music and their place in it.

So, what was it about this group that caught my attention and my "Wow!"?

First, they just start out with such confidence. The opening phrase sings and in so doing lifted me up into the music from the word go. "Now that we have your attention...." That took poise and confidence.

Second, I was aware that this group was comfortable with itself and its musicianship. They are performing at a competition, so they have worked hard to get to this point, but they don't appear in the least bit nervous. They are there and want you to listen to them. They like what they are about to do- and they want you to enjoy it, too. They also trust each other that the other people will do what they are supposed to do.

Third, I noticed that as they played they are aware of each other no matter what is going on. Even when the one moves around to the opposite end the whole group is involved. Their body language throughout let me know that they were playing as a unit. More than a team, the unit moves together with all parts moving smoothly.

Fourth, and I know this may be part of watching on a computer monitor, at times it is difficult to separate which player is playing at any given time. That is part of the movement I mentioned above. But it goes beyond that into the smooth transitions from each musical phrase to the next. The handing-off of the melody is seamless.

Fifth, when they are having to move around, change instruments, adjust the tuning, they do so with class. Part of that is the awareness of each other, but it is also, I think, that they are aware that even when they are not playing, what they do is part of the music. That is an often-overlooked aspect of a public performance. Yes, people are there to listen to the music, but the performers can do things onstage that detract from that. These musicians are very aware of that and work very clearly to keep it to a minimum.

Everything else falls into place for me as I notice these aspects. It allows me to revel in the wonderful sound they present, the fine technique that is always evident, the deep knowledge of the music itself since they are not using music. The entertainment value of the music is enhanced. The success of the group is in their relationship with each other and the music.

Instead of just going "Wow!" I found some things for myself to learn, none of which is profound in and of itself. We all know about working together with others as "teams" and "units." We are all aware that we need to be sensitive to those around us and their part in what we are doing together. We agree that if we do not feel comfortable or competent with what we are doing, we will not succeed. Next time you have a performance with one of your groups, pay attention to how you might look to the people watching you.

I may never play the Toccata and Fugue in a trumpet or brass quintet, but the inspiration of this performance will have an impact on what I do play- and beyond that- to how I interact with people every day.

Chapter 1.5

Inner Music 1

Music is the language of the spirit. It opens the secret of life bringing peace, abolishing strife.

— Kahlil Gibran

More than once on this blog you will find me writing about the "Inner Game." This is based originally on the work of Timothy Gallwey's 1972 classic, *The Inner Game of Tennis.*

Where I want to start in this post is to talk about what is there, inside, where we do the work of the Inner Game. What we find there, I am convinced is the soul, the spirit, that we all have in common but which is expressed in unique ways in each of us. In the midst of that spirit is music, the language of the soul. A large part of what a musician does is get in touch with that inner language and then use the tools of the Inner Game to move that language outward.

We can easily lose this when we think about the music too much. If we try to read it, analyze it, dissect it as if it were a science experiment, we won't hear the music.

When we begin music, it is like learning any language. Whether it was as infants picking up our native tongue or learning a second- or third-language as we got older, we start first with listening and then the basics of the language-notes, time, etc.

Surprisingly (or not) with the language of music it is actually a short jump from "This is a note." to "This is a measure." and on to phrases, songs, and beyond. I watched an instructor and Trumpet Camp take a complete non-trumpet player from nothing to playing a simple song in less than 30 minutes. That included learning how to make the sound.

It was fun to watch. The volunteer was doing this in front of a room full of trumpet players and was somewhat nervous. But in the end, it worked. And we all learned something.

One of the things that I think makes this happen is simply that there is music within us. Our minds, bodies, spirits all respond to music in one way or another. We have an inner rhythm (our heartbeat, for instance) and an awareness of the music around us.

At any level of playing music, we have to hear the inner music in one way or another. With some songs it is easier than others. There is a hook, or phrase that gets our attention. A local composer has written a few marches for our community band. One run through and I found myself humming the tune. I don't know what it is, but he has a way to connect with my inner music, and I guess the inner music of others.

As you work on a musical piece you can be freed to move within the music and no longer be an observer of it. That's part of the inner music- singing it to yourself, reading it as music, not notes on a staff. The desire to "figure it out" through logic or tricks doesn't allow the music to flow.

We aren't used to learning music through the inner music. Brandyn said to me:

> If you think about the next passage instead of just hearing it, you'll create obstacles and that's bad. Just keeping that mindset of singing everything and letting go of everything else is by far the hardest thing and most unfamiliar thing for me to work on. But when we learn how

to do it, it will amaze us. The music we will be able to make will increase drastically each time.

That is where we will look in later posts on the inner game of music. How do we free up this inner music? How does part of us (called Self 1) keep us from doing it and how can we free Self 2 to allow it to happen? It works in all of our lives. The result is musical.

Chapter 1.6

Inner Music 2

People ask me how I make music. I tell them I just step into it. It's like stepping into a river and joining the flow. Every moment in the river has its song
— Michael Jackson

I talked in the last post about "The Inner Game." It began when W. Timothy Gallwey wrote a book in 1974 called *The Inner Game of Tennis.* It was described in a blurb as "a revolutionary program for overcoming the self-doubt, nervousness, and lapses of concentration that can keep a player from winning."

The Inner Game of Music website says

> Instead of serving up technique, it concentrated on the fact that, as Gallwey wrote, "Every game is composed of two parts, an outer game and an inner game." The former is played against opponents, and is filled with lots of contradictory advice; the latter is played not against, but within the mind of the player, and its principal obstacles are self-doubt and anxiety. Gallwey's revolutionary thinking, built on a foundation of Zen thinking and humanistic psychology, was really a primer on how

to get out of your own way to let your best game emerge. It was sports psychology before the two words were pressed against each other and codified into an accepted discipline.
(http://www.innergameofmusic.com/)

Barry Green decided in the mid-1980s to write the first book about the Inner Game that was not about sports. Instead, he applied it to music. Gallwey commented in the introduction that with both sports and music we use the word "play" for things that take a lot of discipline. In music as in sports, "overteaching or overcontrol can lead to fear and self-doubt." Hence the techniques and philosophy of the Inner Game work equally well.

Green tells us then:

> The primary discovery of the Inner Game is that, especially in our culture of achievement-oriented activities, human beings significantly get in their own way. The point of the Inner Game of sports or music is always the same -- to reduce mental interferences that inhibit the full expression of human potential. (Page 7)

We learn in the inner game that there are two "selves" that can be at work in our heads- Self 1 and Self 2. These are not psychological states, personality traits, the conscious and unconscious, right-brain and left-brain, mind and body, or neocortex vs. reptilian brain. They are brain processes that are judged by their impact, the outcome. Simply put by Gallwey and Green:

- If it interferes with your potential, it is Self 1.
- If it enhances your potential, it is Self 2.

> Both Self 1 and Self 2 can access the brain's conscious and unconscious resources, utilize the right- and left-brain styles, or whatever. It's all about the results. (See Green, pp. 16-17)

Gallwey came up with something called The Performance Equation. Green says it this way.

The basic truth is that our performance of any task depends as much on the extent to which we interfere with our abilities as it does on those abilities themselves. This can be expressed as a formula:

$$P = p - i$$

In this equation P refers to Performance, which we define as the result you achieve - what you actually wind-up feeling, achieving and learning, Similarly, p stands for potential, defined as your innate ability -- what you are naturally capable of. And i means interference - you capacity to get in your own way.

Most people try to improve their performance (P) by increasing their potential (p) through practicing and learning new skills.

The Inner Game approach, on the other hand, is to reduce interference (i) at the same time that potential (p) is being trained -- and the result is that our actual performance comes closer to our true potential. (Green, pp. 23 - 24)

He then applies Self 1 and Self 2 to the equation:

- Self 1 is our interference. It contains our concept about how things should be, our judgements and associations. It is particularly fond of the words 'should' and 'shouldn't', and often sees things in terms of what "could have been".
- Self 2 is the vast reservoir of potential within each one of us. It contains our natural talents and abilities, and is a virtually unlimited resource that we can tap and develop. Left to its own devices, it performs with gracefulness and ease. (Green, p. 28)

Which is what we all want as musicians. To be able to play with gracefulness and ease is quite a goal. We all know those moments when it has happened. We also know those many moments when it didn't. Sadly, we often let those less than graceful moments command what we do and how we feel.

When that happens, Self 1 is in full command.

But Green and Gallwey believe that it is possible to work toward a greater role for Self 2 in our lives, and especially in our music.

Inner Game techniques can reduce the effects of self-interference and guide us toward an ideal state of being. This state makes it easier for us to perform at our potential by rousing our interest, increasing our awareness and teaching us to discover and trust our built-in resources and abilities. It is a state in which we are alert, relaxed, responsive and focused. Gallwey refers to it as a state of 'relaxed concentration', and calls it the 'master skill' of the Inner Game. (Green, p. 35)

That's the introduction to the Inner Game. Simply and concisely, it will be a way for us to empower Self 2. Since Self 2 has the same access to our experiences, training, desires, and dreams, it becomes the source of our own empowerment and growth in our skills. It will assist us in dealing with the interference we experience from Self 1.

Of course we have to identify Self 1 when it is taking over. We have to hear that voice and know that it is getting in the way of us doing what we can do.

So for the time being, just become more aware of how your Self 1 voice gets in the way of you doing what you are able to do. Become more able to identify it, even when it makes sense.

In the back of my head, for example, I have an image of an older trumpet player I knew once upon a time. When I knew him, he was probably about the same age I am today, maybe even younger. He was not an accomplished musician. He enjoyed playing, I think, but he had trouble keeping up. His image has always been there in my head as to what happens to amateur trumpet players as they age.

Or, as Self 1 tells me, it's what will happen to me as I age, and there's nothing I can do about it.

Self 2 calls the BS. Self 3 has learned that this is very false. Herb Alpert is over 80. I have more than a decade to get to that. And two decades to catch up to Doc Severinsen who was still performing at 90. I have set Self 1 aside over this past year and went on as if Self 2 were the truth. I am glad I did.

In all of our lives, Self 1 is our inner critic; whom nothing will ever be right. Self 1 will find the faults, the imperfections, the complete lack of possibilities. Don't let Self 1 get in the way of your joy.

Chapter 1.7

Inner Music 3

The nerves are a problem on trumpet, because when you mess up everyone can hear it. Just remember most people are too polite to say anything about it. That should calm your nerves.

-- Wynton Marsalis

In the *Inner Game of Music*, Barry Green adapted the original work of W. Timothy Gallwey. They describe two parts of who we are, Self 1 and Self 2.

- If it interferes with your potential, it is Self 1.
- If it enhances your potential, it is Self 2.

The next part then is to learn and develop three fundamental "inner game" skills to deal with this. Candace Brower on the Albuquerque Music Teacher's blog wrote:

> Green advises us that if we want to reach our full potential as musicians, we need to learn three fundamental skills: (1) awareness, (2)

will, and (3) trust. Awareness is about being fully aware of the sounds, sights, and feelings of playing while avoiding self-judgments that could distort our perceptions. Will is about setting goals, then using the feedback we get from being aware to reach our goals through a process of trial and error. Trust is about letting go of self-judgment and of the physical act of playing to Self 2 and trusting Self 2 to get it right.

I have spent quite a bit of time already on awareness (mindfulness, attention, etc.) and setting goals. What's this thing with trust? Green writes that it is

> Not blind trust, but the trust that comes after hard work, and the trust that comes from knowing there is music inside you....
> In order to achieve our ultimate goal and enter the state of relaxed concentration where we are one with the music, there is one more skill we need. We need to trust ourselves.

Green lists three major obstacles to trust:

- Worries about your self-image,
- The feeling that things are out of your control, and
- Doubts and fears about your own ability.

These feed Self 1's objections to our playing well. Any of these can creep in and interfere with our music. Let's look at each as Green talks about them.

- **Self-image**

"Music is a performing art," says Green. He then says the secret to getting beyond self-image is to give "yourself the character and emotions of the music. You become the music, not yourself." This is like being an actor playing a part. The goal of the actor is to express the character not their own personality. So, it is with music. We come to accept our role as "interpreters of the composer's music."

Okay- easier said than done, especially when we are playing a solo. Our image as a performer can be at stake, we think, if we flub it. If we keep aware of the fact that it is not about us, we are well along the way.

- **Out of control**

Self 1 wants to keep control and make sure everything is going the way it wants. Letting go of control is then the direction to go in our learning. How do we learn to "let go" to Self 2?

That depends on the awareness, goal-setting, and preparation work we have been doing. It is based on trusting ourselves. Why should we trust ourselves? Because we have had years of listening and playing; we have had years of physical training of our embouchure, breathing, fingering; we have been storing all kinds of information in our nervous system to respond when needed. Every one of us has known that moment when we stop worrying and let go to the music. That is the moment when we are in "the groove" - and it works. That's trusting ourselves. We are not in control- and don't need to be- because Self 2 and the music are.

- **Doubting our abilities**

Hard to believe that a trumpet player will ever doubt his or her ability. That sure doesn't match our perceived self-image and personality. But we didn't start out as self-assured about our ability nor do we always have it conquered. But really, what's the worst that could happen? Self 1 will be good at making a catastrophe out of it, but really, what is the worst that is most likely to happen? Chances are it won't be anywhere near as bad as good, old Self 1 thinks.

What's the best that could happen? Probably something far better than the worst. Plus, unless there is a recruiter from the New York Philharmonic or the Canadian Brass sitting in the audience watching you, the best that could happen is most likely the warmth of having done a job well.

Many years ago, my daughter and I were pondering our first ever roller coaster ride. She was 8 or 9 and I was in my early 40s. I had not ridden a coaster in decades; she never. We sat on a bench where we could watch the coaster we were considering. I counted the seconds to the top. (Twenty seconds) I counted the seconds of the first drop. (Three seconds) I timed the whole ride. (2 minutes, 30 seconds) We asked each other the questions about worst and best. Could we survive for those couple seconds it took to drop? (Sure) Would I be way too nervous to bear the tension of the ride to the top? (Who knows?) Would we get sick? (Probably not in those few seconds.) Would we like it? (Probably- but if not, we just don't have to do it again.) We would be completely out of control. (But strapped in.)

We went on the ride.

And then got back in line to do it again. For the next hour as we closed the park. The worst didn't happen, but the best did. We had, in the end, only one real decision to make- did we trust the people who built, maintain, and operate the ride? Just like needing to trust my own ability to play.

Self-trust is the result of our practice and techniques we learn. That crazy run in Tchaikovsky's "Finale to Symphony #4" doesn't look quite as impossible when you realize it is just a variation on all those scales you have been doing for the past years. The solo in Holst's "Song Without Words" from Holst's "Second Suite" isn't quite as scary when you have listened to it for months and done some innovations on how it is constructed and you can see it's form in your mind.

Self-trust. Do you believe you can do it? Have you worked on being able to do it? Have you set goals, formal or informal to be ready to do it? Have you allowed you and the music to meld into a unique idea?

If so, you can do it.

If not, don't quit, just go back and work some more. But remember, sooner or later you will be ready. Do it. You know you can.

The player needs to be able to forget about himself. This is when real communication begins. For with the elimination of the self, he is able to reach the very core of the music, and is free to transmit it.

-Kato Havas

Ms. Brower in the blog post cited above gives a very good counter argument about the seeming "bad guy" status that Green gives to Self 1. She focuses instead on Galleway's original idea that the purpose of the inner game is to bring Self 1 and Self 2 into harmony with each other. (How's that for a good musical idea?) I agree with Ms. Brower and will do some more on this and the insights from neurologists about the brain in the next post.

Chapter 1.8

Inner Music 4

You are only afraid if you are not in harmony with yourself.

— Hermann Hesse

I have written several times about the idea of *The Inner Game of Music,* the book in which Barry Green adapted the original work of W. Timothy Gallwey and tennis to music. Basically, Gallwey and Green describe two parts of who we are, Self 1 and Self 2. Simply put:

- If it interferes with your potential, it is Self 1.
- If it enhances your potential, it is Self 2.

Candace Brower on the Albuquerque Music Teacher's blog wrote about three fundamental skills for the "Inner Game": (1) awareness, (2) will, and (3) trust. With inspiration from Ms. Brower has written as well as science's increased knowledge of how the brain works, let me move to a new dimension of the inner game.

It would be easy to read the books and come to a logical conclusion as pointed out by Ms. Brower:

- Self 1 is the bad guy, the enemy;
- Self 2 is the good guy, the hero.

Which is too much of a black and white dichotomy for Brower and for me. Green seems to be telling us that all we have to do is get rid of Self 1 and give Self 2 free reign. We will then flourish, bloom, become great. (Overstatement on purpose!) Brower asks the question:

> ...does Self 2 really have what it takes to learn the refined skills of playing a musical instrument or to perform a complex piece of music from memory? None of us is born with the innate ability to play a musical instrument, and in fact, it requires many years of training, and the development of very precise motor skills.

She goes on:

> ... I have found it helpful to recast the relationship between Self 1 and Self 2 in more positive terms that align it more closely both with Timothy Gallwey's original conception and with what neuroscientists have since learned about the brain and nervous system. In The Inner Game of Tennis, Gallwey does not demonize Self 1, but rather encourages us to "improve the relationship" between Self 1 and Self 2. According to Gallwey, harmony [emphasis added] between Self 1 and Self 2 comes not when Self 1 disappears, but when Self 1 becomes quiet and focused, so that the "two selves are one."

Without going into all the advances and insights in neuroscience that inform and affirm this, let me simplify it very quickly.

Self 1 is seated in the thinking, decision-making part of the brain. It is hard at work doing its essential tasks when we are learning something. It is an essential part of the learning process. As we practice and repeat the new skills, the actions move deeper into the brain. We have heard people talk about "muscle memory", for example. This is when the less conscious and pre-conscious parts of the brain have taken over the activities. This is Self 2. When Self 1 begins to see that Self 2 knows what to do, Self 1 is free to learn the next thing. Hence, we improve our skills, move on to more complex activities, etc.

Ms. Brower's thoughts tell us that the skills of awareness, will, and trust are learned by Self 1! That is not what Self 2 is able to do. She continues:

> It is Self 1 who must be aware and set goals, and who must learn to trust Self 2. If Self 1 cannot let go of self-judgment, driven by the need to win the approval of others, this can get in the way of performing the many other tasks that it needs to carry out.

Self 1 and Self 2 are not adversaries but collaborators working together in a spirit of cooperation. As a teacher she helps her students sort out which tasks belong to Self 1 and which to Self 2, so their two selves can work together to master the complex skills of playing a musical instrument. (Article no longer posted. Originally retrieved in 2015. Albuquerque Music Teacher's blog.)

How does this work? Here's an example from any experience with playing music:

Technique: Scales and Key Signatures

- We learn and practice up and down the scales.
- We look at that key signature and use Self 1 to name what the flats and sharps are.
- We then play that scale. In doing that we are learning the relationships between the different notes through hearing and seeing, at least at the beginning, the notes on the page.
- We begin to learn consciously that this is the movement of our fingers, embouchure, air, etc. as we play this particular scale starting on whatever note we begin with.

Months and years later we are playing a piece written in that key. Self 1 pays attention, appropriately, to the key signature. It tells Self 2, "Go for it. It's now in your hands." Experience has taught us that we know the key and how to play it. Self 2 takes over and does what is needed to play in that key.

Self 1 relaxes. It remains aware, mindful, ready to catch things like key changes, accidentals, particular rhythms, etc. Then Self 2 goofs. (We are, after all, human.) This is a new piece and as we were playing, Self 2 misses that F# or Eb of the key. Not a big deal. It is practice or rehearsal. So, what do we do? Self 1 jumps back in and reminds us. We stop and circle that note. Self 1 is overriding the automatic mistake of Self 2. Self 2 is still in control. It is the driver. But Self 1 has become the navigator, as Brower describes it. The circle around the note becomes a navigation aid. Self 1 catches that and immediately sends the message through Self 2- play the sharp or flat.

The work of the brain and mind, Self 1 and Self 2, in tandem, each doing their appropriate tasks.

- Collaboration is at work- just as between ourselves and the other musicians in whatever group we are participating with. Now, though the collaboration is with ourselves! The three skills of the "inner game" are being utilized effectively.
- Awareness is at work- the mindfulness to what is happening around us in tone, style, etc.
- Will is at work- Self 1 has done its job setting goals and guiding the process to get where it is today.
- Trust is at work- or the collaboration wouldn't be happening. Self 1 knows Self 2 is competent. Fear is reduced allowing for harmony as the Hesse quote above notes.
- Harmony is the result- music is being made.

Circling around then we have the same concerns we have always had as well as the same answers. Not to be too cliched about it but it does boil down to

- practice and
- how we practice.

Simple.
Now we have to do it.

Chapter 1.9

Efficiency and Planning

Musical training is a more potent instrument than any other, because rhythm and harmony find their way into the inward places of the soul.

— Plato, The Republic

Let me start with a confession... Sometimes we write about things that we aren't doing in order to make ourselves research them and then, if the stars align correctly and the rivers don't flood, we may actually try what we are talking about. In other words, I am not good at this week's topic:

Efficiency and planning in practice.

I never have been. I don't believe I am alone. Most of us play instruments because we want to play music. Long tones, then playing scales or chromatics, endless lip slurs begins to sound boring. At best. So, we collect song books, method books, lesson books, etudes, etc. in the vain hope that the more we have to choose from the more likely we will be to actually play them.

Sure, we have Arban's, Clarke, and Schlossberg. We may even have tried to put together some routine out of them. We are good for a while and then get sidetracked by any one of a number of things.

At Trumpet Camp in August, we all received a handout that had the start of a decent daily routine. I added some Arban's and Schlossberg to it and soon was in the groove of regular practice. With the exception of a period in September when circumstances were beyond my control, I have been doing quite well.

The result is as expected. My range, tone, style, technique, and endurance have almost skyrocketed. But the efficiency is beginning to wane. I am now finding myself being distracted as I am playing long tones or missing fingering on chromatics that we all have played for years.

In other words, I may be playing my trumpet, but I am not practicing as efficiently as I did in mid-August and I am not playing musically. Some days I do slurs, other days sight-reading. One day I will work through scale exercises and the next play rhythm challenges. Am I getting better? Sure. My embouchure is improving and my tone is the best it's probably ever been. But I'm just kind of wandering around the practice. I am only now beginning to ask, "What is it I need to be working on?"

I went surfing and searching on the Web to see what's out there. Let me start with a list from Wynton. (Do I need to give his last name?)

THE WYNTON MARSALIS 12 RULES OF EFFECTIVE PRACTICE:

1. Seek out the best private instruction you can afford.
2. Write/work out a regular practice schedule.
3. Set realistic goals.
4. Concentrate when practicing
5. Relax and practice slowly
6. Practice what you can't play. - (The hard parts.)
7. Always play with maximum expression.
8. Don't be too hard on yourself.
9. Don't show off.
10. Think for yourself. - (Don't rely on methods.)
11. Be optimistic. - "Music washes away the dust of everyday life."
12. Look for connections between your music and other things.

(http://ojtrumpet.net/practice/WYNTON_MARSALIS_RULES.html)

What then, to look at numbers two and three on Wynton's list, should my schedule look like? What do I need to develop?

Here's a place to start on schedule and planning as found on The Trumpet Studio:

> Begin working on a particular skill (tonguing, scales, range) in simple, attainable steps, then increasing the difficulty SLIGHTLY. Practicing that level for many repetitions UNTIL MASTERED, then increasing the difficulty. It may take hours, days or weeks to MASTER a particular level. Mastery is obtained when you can play a particular passage or selection 10-15 times at the given metronome marking with no mistakes. (https://www.trumpetstudio.com/skill.html)

This doesn't happen overnight. On the Trumpet Studio the plan is to move from single to double-tonguing mastery in up to 6 months, moving across all the scales. That picks up on Wynton's #5- practice slowly, which can also expand into "Practice patiently."

What are the essentials of my becoming a more efficient and capable trumpet player? I need to look at what I can already do and see where the growth needs to happen. A year ago, I decided to work hard at sight-reading, one of my poorer skills. I got the Getchell *2nd Book of Practical Studies* and just started working through it. (No, I wasn't very organized at it. I just kept playing the next exercise until I reached the end- and then started over.) Did it work? Yep. Could it have worked better if I hadn't been impatient? Yep. Am I happy with where it took me? Yep. Could I continue to do better? You bet.

But that "better" will be more than just sight-reading. It will be in technique as I learn to play the dynamics and tone of the pieces. But the days I work too much on that, I don't do scales or slurs. There's always a trade-off. That brings me back to the scheduling and deciding what my goals are to be. Which takes me to #1 on the list- an instructor/teacher. Yes, I have had them. But I have not been able to use them as effectively as possible.

See how it gets complicated and how someone like me who is not Mr. Organization can get turned off to practicing and end up getting nowhere?

Let me challenge me (and you), then, to begin to make a list of the goals we want to achieve in the next few months. Let's talk to our instructors about ways to move forward. Agree to a schedule but don't be so rigid that you get angry if you miss it by a day or even hour.

This is supposed to be fun.

And make sure you take time to play music. After all, that's why we practice.

Which, as I have said before, is a lot like life. And as ever, more to come as these continue to develop.

Chapter 1.10

All Life is a Privilege

The wise musicians are those who play what they can master

-Duke Ellington

It is so easy to think we are deserving of what we have and what we can get. It is a trap to believe that we are entitled to something, or have worked hard enough to have earned it.

Somewhere in the middle of trumpet camp, director Bob Baca made the comment to us:

- Everything is a privilege. We don't deserve any of it.

We all shook our heads in some kind of understanding. It made some kind of sense. We don't "deserve" it.

As I started writing this week's post I decided to think more about the word "privilege" and was surprised to be reminded that the word can be very loaded with negative connotations.

Here are three ways to define "privilege." These are from the Merriam-Webster Dictionary and show how it can certainly be a negative idea:

- a right or benefit that is given to some people and not to others
- the advantage that wealthy and powerful people have over other people in a society
- a special opportunity to do something that makes you proud. (www. merriam-webster.com/dictionary/privilege)

Using the word "privilege" begins to sound like an entitlement some people expect or get simply because of who they are. It is a special "right" that not everyone has and that can easily be used to put others down or elevate ourselves more highly than we ought to.

But that's not where I want to go with this. That's not what was meant when we were told that "Everything is a privilege." In reality, the word privilege when used in this was is actually a humbling word.

Let's look at the last one of the above definitions for our purposes here this week:

- a special opportunity to do something that makes you proud
- I would expand that a little by using several examples:
- I have been privileged to have known a number of deeply committed people in my life.
- I have been privileged to be allowed to help other people in my work.
- I have been privileged to be part of an amazing group that helps others.

All these recognize that not everyone may have had the same "privileges" as I have, but these are not mine because of something I am or who I am or even what I have done. I have been given the honor of doing these things.

That humbles me since it is not by my good works or special talents that have allowed me this honor. Many times, it may simply be that I was in the right place at the right time.

What does this have to do with my trumpet playing? How could this impact how I play, practice, or interact with others?

For me it starts with the awareness that the opportunities I have to be a musician start out as a privilege. Not everyone has these opportunities nor does everyone want them. I have been fortunate to have the opportunities, the time, (hopefully) the talent to do something wonderful like making music. It does not make me any more special than anyone else. It is simply what I have been given and worked at developing.

The key to that is to then remember that when I face someone who may have different skills or interests than I do. It means accepting the musician who is better than I am- and supporting the one who is not as good as I am. It puts me in the better position of not having to prove anything- or disprove anything. I can simply be the player- and person I am.

It also means that I am also being given the privilege from time to time to give to others of what I have been given. Through my music in the different groups I play with, I am giving to those listening and to those who play in the group with me, a piece of myself. If I believe that music is as important as I say it is, it is humbling to be able to share in whatever ways possible with others. The opportunities are endless.

But I am also privileged to receive from my co-musicians as we make the music together. It is all a give and take. When I live as if all I have is a privilege, I can make a difference in my own life as well as the lives of others.

Like everything else, and as I always seem to be saying- that's a lot like life.

Chapter 1.11

Bloom

Blow your life through your horn.

Arturo Sandoval

One could ask, who else's life could you blow through the horn? Well, sadly, many times we try to be something or someone we are not. We can have role models, but we can't be them. We can wish for other times or places, but we only have what we have in front of us.

Over 55 years ago I attended my first professional, big-time concert. It was August 1966 and I had just graduated from high school. I had been playing trumpet for almost four years, had achieved first chair status the previous year, and played in a local "garage band" that covered Tijuana Brass music.

That first concert I ever went to was at the Allentown Fair in Allentown, PA, and featured my hero- Herb Alpert and the Tijuana Brass. (Sergio Mendez and Brazil '66 opened for them with their lead singer, Lani Hall.) I was in heaven.

A few months later the TJB came out with their seventh album, S.R.O. and there on the back was a picture taken at that concert!

Jump ahead by 49 years and 2 months to 2015. That 18-year-old trumpeter (me) is now a 67-year-old trumpeter, probably better than I ever was. The trumpet player on-stage is now an 80-year-old trumpet player with a new album just released and in the middle of a concert tour.

Both of us are still playing, Lani Hall, now his wife, is still singing... and I had the pleasure and exciting honor of attending their concert and meeting him at Rochester's Riverside Live! Concert series.

Herb Alpert is also better than ever.

While this is not a review of the show, I will say that it was amazing and far more than would be expected. His ability at the trumpet is outstanding and his sense of music-making is better than ever. He plays jazz in a number of different styles, engages the audience in questions and answers, and is having a great time. He is doing this, I am sure, because he likes it. Music is his life and he needs to share it, on-stage, with others. He doesn't need to do this- he likes doing it.

That's part of the "who" of Herb Alpert. He tips his hat to the music that made him famous with a medley of TJB music, but that's not the highlight of the show. The Tijuana Brass is who he WAS. Many other artists would capitalize on that old music. Alpert is not interested in that. He wants to entertain with who he IS.

He capitalizes on his skill and the ability to do what he does with style and professionalism. He is not a "screaming" trumpet player. He takes the horn and makes the music that he knows he can make with presence and quality. Within that he uses all the notes of the horn in his solid range. At age 80 he utilizes the wisdom he has acquired over decades of making music to enhance his style and move it forward.

Within the solid range of the trumpet, he advances the music as both confident soloist and self-assured leader of the quartet. He plays standards then improvises and innovates. He trades fours with the drummer who moves into an extended solo that Alpert returns to as it falls into place.

That is the "where" of Herb Alpert- the here and now. Someone from the audience asked him who he wished he had played with and he commented that he had the opportunity to play with Miles Davis. But he added that he didn't feel it was right. That wasn't who he was. (I would disagree, but then I am a fan of both of them.)

One can listen to Maynard Ferguson and try to be a "screamer." But without the skill and "chops," doing that will become a disaster. One can try to continually repeat what used to be. That, too, wouldn't work.

Being real- being oneself- is what life is really all about. It shows up on the trumpet, but it also shows up at home in our families and at work with colleagues as well as in whatever we try to do on a daily basis. If I try to be someone I cannot be- or someone I once was- it will not be real.

Who am I?

Where am I in my life's growth?

How can I use my here and now skills and resources to keep moving forward into whatever comes next?

Answer those questions- every day. Seek to build on where you were yesterday, moving into where you want to be tomorrow, by doing what you can do today!

I sat in humility watching and listening to Alpert, but he also encouraged me by still doing what he does better than ever.

We do not stop innovating because we have gotten older; we do not stop improving what we can do because we don't have the same skills as someone else. We can each find our place regardless of age, skill, or time.

If you are young, take heart that you haven't reach the pinnacle of what you can be. Keep at it. What does Herb Alpert do when he is not on a concert tour or on days he performs? He does scales. The simple, basic building blogs of all that we do. Scales. (I am sure he does a lot of other things, too, but he builds that on the basics.)

So, Herb Alpert, thank you for growing and still performing, clearly enjoying life and taking time to greet me and remind me what life is all about.

Chapter 1.12

No Wandering

On those long notes behind the trumpet solo, if anyone lets his mind wander for a minute he is dead.

-Don Ellis

Things are moving along nicely. You are in "the groove." You are feeling what the rest of the group is doing. It can be a concert band piece or a trio. You know the music is working its magic on you and you couldn't feel better.

Then for a moment you get distracted. It could be something out of the corner of your eye or a note that didn't land just right from you or someone else. Maybe you just remembered something you forgot to do before you left home. Perhaps a memory of another performance was triggered by a note or just a random thought drifted up from the unconscious.

Suddenly the whole mood and feel changes. You aren't lost- you know right where you are, but the groove is gone. You are not in sync with what's happening. If you are in a concert band you may get away with it. If you are in the midst of a solo, as great trumpet player Don Ellis so bluntly put it- you're dead.

Now, I know Robert Baca said the same thing about "panic." The truth is, though, it's true. It took me years to realize the truth of it- and why my performances were often riddled with moments when I "died." No one noticed most of them except perhaps the director and the person sitting next to me. But distraction is for me the worst of.....

Squirrel.

Just kidding. Another way of describing this result of distraction is that obstacles appear when we take our mind away from the sound, the music, or the goal. Obstacles are things that get in the way of doing what we want to or are usually able to do. When I have listened to recordings of some of my solos in the big band or concert band, I have often noticed one thing in particular- the sound. Perhaps it is better to say that I notice when my "sound" goes flat or isn't alive. The obstacle is not that I can't keep a clearer sound, the obstacle is maintaining it when I am distracted.

Sometimes I get distracted by the fact that I just did the previous line or phrase better than usual. I take that moment to congratulate myself- and I am distracted. Sometimes I get distracted by paying too much attention to the audience and I get flustered. Sometimes in life I get distracted by "the small stuff" and miss the goals and hopes I have for myself.

Even good things can be distractions, of course. If it takes me away from my goals, it is a distraction.

High-wire artist, acrobat, and daredevil Nik Wallenda of the famous Flying Wallendas has this to say:

I've trained all my life not to be distracted by distractions.

Nik Wallenda

Perhaps what Wallenda does is maintain focus and be mindful. Staying in the moment is essential. Notice that he says he has had to "train" all his life to do it. I do not think it comes naturally. We are easily distracted because that is how our brain is constructed. It is part of the ancient survival system. To learn how to do this takes time and energy.

We learn in the practice room when we work on our pieces so that we know them more than just technically. We learn focus as we become familiar with the rhythms and flow that make the music alive. We learn mindfulness as we take the time to sing the parts out loud to feel the movement. We discover awareness as we listen to ourselves play and how what we are playing fits into the greater picture of the music.

But we also improve our musical focus ability when we take five or ten minutes on a daily basis to meditate or focus on our breathing as a way of bringing ourselves back into the moment. What we do in the hours of the day when we are not playing music can have a huge impact on how we learn to avoid distractions. Our music is not a box we can separate from the rest of our lives. Nor is our life a separate box from the music.

As we learn to integrate who we are and what we do, we find that our music will flow from us.

And we can flow from our music.

Practice mindfulness. Stay in the moment. Pay attention to your breath. Feel the pulse of the music as you play. Remember the sound you want and play it. Don't think about it; don't analyze it. In your practice - just play it so it is yours.

Chapter 1.13

Panic and Air

If you panic, you will die.

-R. Baca

A couple years ago I was doing a hike near Lake Itasca here in Minnesota. There was this circular trail around a lake that branched off the main trail. Or, at least is felt like that. In reality it was just a loop that came back to the same spot and then back out. The problem was that at the spot where the trail started the loop, the two sides of the loop were almost parallel to each other. So, as I returned to the point where the loop started, I found myself facing a "Y" and I didn't know which way to turn. I turned left and realized I was passing things I already passed in the same direction. So I turned around and got back to the "Y" and turned right. Yep- wrong again. I was now heading up the loop from the other side. I wasn't sure of this until I got to a place where I took some pictures of a beaver dam.

By this time, I am already later than I expected to be in getting back to the car. My wife would certainly be getting worried. (She was.) We were out in the wilderness and the GPS on my iPhone wasn't showing any map. I knew I wasn't lost. But I knew I could become like Winnie-the-Pooh going in circles around the same tree. The only lesson I could think of at that time was an old hiking reminder:

Don't panic! Your life may depend on it.

I am not sure I was quite at "panic" level on the trail, but I was beginning to get concerned. I thought I knew what I was doing. But it was getting warm, I was getting a little tired. How was I going to deal with this?

I stopped, took a deep breath or two, calmed my mind and set about figuring out that I needed just to be more observant of what I was doing. It worked.

When Bob Baca said the quote at the top of this post at Trumpet Camp it resonated. It applies to playing the trumpet, as much as it applies to hiking Itasca Park. Don't panic.

We can sure panic when we aren't prepared to play that solo in tomorrow's concert. We can panic when we get lost in the middle of a complicated (or easy) piece in the band's gig. Maybe we're in the midst of the show and our lip decides to quiver and rebel. What are we to do?

First and foremost: Don't panic. It will work against you. We have developed quite a system for survival over the years of our human evolution. the "panic" response is one of them. Panic, or anxiety, can happen when we are facing a "dangerous" or even "life-threatening" situation. Way back in our human development such anxiety or panic got all the systems moving in order for us to survive.

We can call it today the "Fight, Flight, or Freeze" response.

But that quivering lip, the un-prepared solo or jumped line in a song is not life-threatening. Our response is just a left-over. But we can easily metaphorically "die" if we allow the panic to take over. The extra adrenaline pumping with an elevated blood-pressure moving blood away from the thinking brain so we react intuitively makes it more likely that we will not get through the panic. The solo will fail, we won't find our spot in time for our next entrance, the quivering lip just gets work.

But there is another response that we can learn and cultivate. Instead of fight, flight, or freeze, we can learn "Flow." As in "Go with the flow!" I don't know who T. McIrvine is, but I found this quote from him online about playing the trumpet.

**Release the air,
don't blow the air.**

This is, of course, good advice at all times, which I may talk about some other time. For today, though, this is a great way to think when facing those moments of panic. Stop and breathe. No, not that short, panting breath or that heavy rush of air as if you were blowing out the candles on your 100th birthday cake. Something more relaxed, conscious.

Let's put these things together: Panic and air. Take it easy. Allow the air to fill from the diaphragm. Count to five as you are inhaling through the nose. Hold for a count of two. Count to six as you slowly exhale, letting the air move from your stomach. Do this a couple of times. Don't focus on anything but your breathing. (Autocorrect wanted to make that say, "you're" breathing. I realized that both are correct. It is yours; notice it! "You are" breathing. Notice that, too!)

Can you do this while playing? Probably not to its fullest, but look for several measures of rest. Then do it. You won't revitalize your quivering lip, but you will loosen the tension that only makes the quivering worse. Pay attention to the ease of playing- letting the air release through the mouthpiece and around through the horn. It may be just enough to get you through the rest of the gig.

In your practice on that day before the concert, it will slow you down enough to figure out what you need to do.

Getting rid of the panic response will reconnect you to the music and you will more easily recognize where you might be in the music. After all, you have been practicing and you know the piece, right?

Lots of ways breathing can work for us, not just making a better sound. Perhaps good breathing exercises should be in our regular routine. Long tones, of course, can help with that as can "releasing" air through the lead tube without the tuning slide. But regular daily meditative, mindful breathing may do as much for our tone and music as scales. (BOTH are important, of course.)

As we learn to breathe, life itself can be a lot easier to come with.

Here's a closing quote from a new book I just came across:

Sometimes it's okay if the only thing you did today was breathe.
                    -Yumi Sakugawa, There's No Right Way to Meditate

Chapter 1.14

Keeping the Soul in the Music

Music in the soul can be heard by the universe.

— Lao Tzu

We went to another "big name" concert last weekend, the second in a month. This time it was country music star and daughter of Johnny Cash, Rosanne Cash. No, there were no trumpets with her but I spent a lot of time being mindful of her performance and what I can learn from it about performing and playing trumpet. Some were additions to what I saw and experienced with Herb Alpert in the previous concert. Others were new. So here goes...

Overarching the whole experience was the awareness that these people play this music day after day. How in the world can they keep the music alive in countless performances? How can they make it feel as fresh for this night as they did 20 or 30 concerts ago? Hence the title of this post reflects the question of keeping the "soul" in the music for every performance.

Rosanne did it beautifully. The power behind her singing was as soulful as anyone. The words to her songs took the music to new depths - and vice versa. So, in a sense, one way to keep the music alive is the way you plan the show.

Cash is doing something unusual on this tour. She is performing her most recent album, *The River and the Thread*, in full and as recorded on the CD. She gave the background of the album and thoughts about each song, putting it into context and giving us a glimpse of her writing. It took about an hour or so and was the first half of the concert. I would say it was one of the more remarkable concert experiences I have ever witnessed. She never lost her soul. She connected with the audience and brought us into her world.

How do I do that when in performance? How does my brass quintet, for example, allow the audience to participate as more than a passive listener? Even though they are there for the music, what else can we bring to them. Both Cash and Alpert at the earlier concert do that through their interactions with the audience. Alpert took questions and responded to people's interest; Cash took us behind the music to allow the meaning of the songs touch us differently.

In our quintet or big band, as the designated announcer, I take the time between songs, if it isn't a dance with the big band, to tell the stories of the songs. I put them into context, their history, explain why we play them or perhaps how they showcase a quintet or big band. Some of that is covering for music changes, but it is also to bring the audience, metaphorically on stage with us. But it is also about my keeping my focus on the music's soul. I am reminding myself of the music's inner life, our inner lives as musicians, and why we are doing what we are doing.

On stage interactions are another set of issues for bands in performance. At the Cash concert I overheard two different responses to what was happening on stage. First was one person commenting that they enjoyed watching the musicians during the songs- what they are doing, different tricks and movements, how *they* are responding to the music. You will see how the drummer exaggerates certain movements to give a different emphasis, the keyboardist fiddling with the controls getting just the right sound, the guitarists closing their eyes and letting the music flow from their fingers.

For the audience that part of the show is just as real as the person doing the lead. If the band is not engaged, is just going through the motions and playing the notes, the overall experience will be diminished.

That was the second response I heard about the Cash show- the band seemed tired; they weren't as alive as Cash herself. I'm not entirely sure I saw that as much as the person I was talking to did. I wondered if some of the group just knew they weren't the stars so they tried to stay in the background? It didn't seem to me to diminish their performance.

But it does raise issues for any of us as performing musicians.

What do you do in your band when another person or section is soloing? Are you engaged or are you sitting or standing there looking bored? Do you give the impression that when it is not centered on you or your part that it isn't worth paying attention to? That can happen so easily since we are concerned about the next part or the water gurgling in the horn. Be aware, though, of how the audience responds to that as well.

We play music for a reason- it is a soul experience. We do it because we are moved by it. In the end it will come to some performance. We are charged, at that point as performing musicians to communicate to the audience that soul experience. Whether you are the lead trumpet soaring on a solo or the 4th section musician doing little more than "oom pahs" your part is important- as is your interactions with the music. Your soul is part of the whole. Feel it and live it through the horn and your engagement with the rest of the band.

Again, as it seems to always be, the connection to life is hopefully obvious. How do you relate to the world around you? Do you engage or do you go through life with a sense of disinterest if it isn't centered on you? What do you have to offer in even the smallest ways to the soul of the situation?

Find your soul and then let it be lived.

Chapter 1.15

Perception is Reality

Don't be afraid, just play the music.

— Charlie Parker

As a counselor, one thing I always have to keep in mind is that when someone sees reality a certain way, they believe it. For them it IS reality. It doesn't matter whether it is true or imagined. Reality is often what we perceive it to be. When they come into my office or group for therapy I have to start where they are- even if I know it to be false or mis-perceived.

As we pick up our horn to practice or to perform, what we consider reality will govern what we do next.

For years I believed I could not play a solo.

I was right. I couldn't play a solo. I would always mess it up. Even though I kept at it in church, for example, if I had a organ or piano and trumpet duet I never, ever got it right. Never. Something would always go wrong. I would miss a count and therefore come in early or late. I would miss a sharp or flat and play a discordant note. Any one of a number of things happened every time. Most people didn't notice it as significant most of the time, but I did.

"See," I would say to myself, "you can't play a solo."

I was proving the truth of Henry Ford's statement:

> *Whether you think you can,*
> *or you think you can't--*
> *you're right.*

Fortunately, I loved playing trumpet so much I never allowed it to stop me from trying or from continuing to play in bands. I would avoid solos, even in band. My trumpet soloing with even 55 other musicians would send my heart into high gear, the adrenaline would flow, the fight or flight mechanism would kick in- and I would mess it up.

Over and over the refrain- you can't solo, you can't solo, you can't!

My perception of reality was true- even if it wasn't.

Note that this was not a fear of being in front of people. I have been in public for 50 years preaching, radio DJ, cable TV host. I could stand and talk to hundreds of people and not be nervous. Put a trumpet in my hand and make me solo in front of a handful- forget it. I can't do that. So said my perception of reality.

What happened, especially since I wouldn't be writing about it if it hadn't changed?

My first step was to work with a teacher. Just to play in his presence was a big step. He gave me some assignments; I worked on them; I improved.

Second, I was invited to join a brass quintet. When there are only five of you, each part is, in essence, a solo. We had a lot of fun practicing and developing a repertoire. When we finally did play in public performance I did okay, but I still messed up somewhere in each performance. Again, not always noticeable and never as badly as I had before, but I was building confidence in myself- and reality was shifting.

Third, I began playing some first parts in our community band. I found that most of the time I could do that! But that wasn't a solo. Again- perceptions were changing internally.

Fourth, one year ago this week the community band had a concert and with a solo on one number. My teacher was also playing first and he told me that I was playing it. I didn't argue. I figured that if he thought I was capable, maybe I was.

We worked on it in my lessons. I could play it very well- at home or in the lesson. But not at any rehearsal. Never.

I can't play solos!

But I refused to back down. (Stubborn ol' cuss!) The director never suggested I give it to someone else. The night before the concert we had our dress rehearsal and ...

Nope, still not right.

Concert night. The piece comes up. ("Valdres March" by Hanssen) It starts with my trumpet solo. I do okay. A little week. Maybe I can solo? Maybe?

We get to the end and approach the D.C. back to the top- and the solo. One last chance. As we move along toward the D.C. I have a conversation with myself.

- This music is supposed to be fun.
- You're not having fun.
- Have fun.
- You can do it.
- Screw it.
- Play the damn thing!!!

Yep- it worked.

I nailed it. My teacher gave me a thumbs up!

The first solo I felt I played well in almost 50 years.

Reality made a seismic shift and I was now a "real" trumpet player again.

After the first of the year, I will be doing some posts on the idea of "The Inner Game" about how we sabotage ourselves with a "Self-One" and a "Self-Two". That's what this is really about. It starts with our perception of reality. What we believe is what guides us. Reality or not, if we see it that way, that's the way it is. Don't confuse me with facts.

Unless you want to learn to do it differently. I didn't realize that's what I was doing when I started this journey about five or six years ago; when I said yes to the quintet or decided to take lessons again.

So,

- Get out of yourself and seek support and new insights.
- Stretch yourself. Take some chances and risks. All you can do is make a mistake. It's not the end of the world.
- Keep practicing.
- Hear the perception of reality that is keeping you from doing what you can do.
- Then do it.

That's what I did over the years in my life. It works with any task I think I can or can't do. The trumpet isn't any different.

And it is supposed to be fun. Enjoy it!

(BTW: Thanks to Warren, Steve, and Mike for sticking with me through these past years!)

Chapter 1.16

In Gratitude

Gratitude is the music of the heart.

-Unknown

It's Thanksgiving Week and it is hard to move past the week without talking about gratitude.

Will gratitude make you a better musician? Not as much as practice will, but it will do something just as important that will have an impact- it will increase your mindfulness, your awareness of yourself and the world around you. THAT will help your trumpet playing.

- It will give you insight into your own life and emotions- an important part of being an advancing musician.
- It will keep you in touch with those around you that will make your life fuller and more enriching.
- It will keep you humble- which is another way of saying you will continue to be teachable- willing and ready to learn.

- It will increase your happiness levels on a daily basis, say a number of research studies.
- It will increase your energy and motivation more often.
- Depression and stress will be more easily coped with on a daily basis.

As preachers have been saying for years on Thanksgiving, don't just save all your gratitude for this one day. It actually will make you a better person if you learn to practice it every day.

- Dr. Amit Sood, formerly of Mayo Clinic suggests that you not get out of bed in the morning any day without some awareness of reasons or people to be grateful for. (stressfree.org/)
- Keep a gratitude journal and review it on a daily basis.
- Don't repeat yourself- find new reasons to be grateful each day.
- Silently wish each person you pass in a given period of time, grace and peace.
- Meister Eckhart was a man of wisdom:

If the only prayer you say in your life is 'thank you,'
that would suffice.

One person who has helped me over the past couple years is Shane Burcaw. He is a young man with Spinal Muscular Atrophy and has been in a wheelchair his whole life. He also has a journalism degree, is the author of a wonderful book, *Laughing at My Nightmare*, is the founder of a foundation to assist others with Muscular Dystrophy and its variations, and has an incredible sense of humor. His attitude is nothing short of remarkable. No, he does not play trumpet (I don't think so, anyway!) but he is a person filled with energy- and gratitude. (https://laughingatmynightmare.tumblr.com/about)

Every week he posts a list called *What Made Me Smile This Week*. There are many things each week that bring a smile to Shane's face: meeting with college students at his Alma Mater (Moravian College!), eating turkey chili, giving a talk at an elementary school, writing, or just being able to stretch out after a long day. Each week he makes me smile. He also reminds me of the wonders I miss around me when all I do is complain or find reasons to criticize. He challenges me, someone nearly three times his age, to see the world as fresh and refreshing each day. No matter what!

Maybe I should apply that to my trumpet playing and practice. How did my practicing today make me smile? What were the moments of gratitude and joy? Maybe I wasn't as focused as I needed to be, but what was neat about it? Maybe it was the particular exercise that is just fun to play. Maybe it was the ability to hit some difficult notes with a little more clarity. Maybe it was just the way I felt after making music.

What works for you? Where are you grateful today? Just enjoy it. No matter what!

Chapter 1.17

Sky Thinking

Hard work beats talent when talent doesn't work hard.

-Tim Notke

I'm actually not going to write about "hard work" but about what I may need in order to do the "hard work." That happens to be having "goals." In essence goals are the ways we know where we are going. Over the years I have been taught at many workshops that goals have to be SMART:

- Specific – target a specific area for improvement.
- Measurable – quantify or at least suggest an indicator of progress.
- Attainable – assuring that an end can be achieved.
- Realistic – state what results can realistically be achieved, given available resources.
- Time-related – specify when the result(s) can be achieved.

-Wikipedia

Which means that my goal

to be an excellent trumpet player

doesn't really fit the criteria. But

to be able to play at speed the first section (12 measures) of Arban's 1st Characteristic Study by January 15

Does fit. I have a few goals related to next summer's Big Band and Trumpet Camps, including

to be able to comfortably extend my range to that elusive (to me) high C or D

as well as

to be more comfortable with dealing with changes in songs and do an improvised solo.

That goal of comfort in changes is a little too vague to really fit the criteria. If I have some specific activities and exercises that I am using to get in that direction such a long-range goal can tend to be okay.

The *Edge of Unachievable* is one way we learned at camp to find goals. Go to the edge of what you can't achieve- and chances are you will go beyond it. Maybe we could also use the phrase *Sky Thinking*. Even though that phrase is often used to mean things that are out of touch with reality, why do our goals have to be that way? How about, instead, the goals may be on the edge of unachievable but not quite out of reach. With hard work informing and forming whatever talent we may have, who says we can't get there?

Hoping your Sky Thinking plans have been Written Down, and traced back to exactly what to Act on today.

-Bob Baca

Expanding on Bob Baca's wish for us at the end of camp, there are three things necessary for us to move forward.

Do your sky thinking. Brainstorm. Take some time to think about where you want to be in a month, six months. I was talking to a young trumpet player the other week who has been working on the "Carnival of Venice" from Arban's. He has already played it for Solo/Ensemble but hasn't reached where he wants to go with it. He is still pushing his sky thinking.

Write them down. Start a journal where you note your sky thinking goals and can see your progress. If they aren't written down, they are less likely to happen. The further out you go, of course, the less specific you can be. You also have to be ready to go with whatever life may throw at you. Don' be so rigid that you will break if something gets in your way. Writing them down may also be a way to share them with others- teachers, family, friends, band directors- who can help you.

Translate into action. Ah, here's the work. I am great at spinning ideas and plans into thin air (the "sky" of sky thinking.) I can easily get side-tracked by those pesky squirrels that are everywhere. I can lose focus and direction if I don't have some form of plan of action. It doesn't have to be fully outlined with footnotes and explanations. I'm not that structured. But I need a flow-chart that keeps me on the ball. *I need to have some way of knowing what I need to do today in order to get closer to my goal tomorrow.*

Put this all together and I end up with a far better set of goals than I had when I started. I also feel better about what I am doing. I know I am going somewhere that I can regularly test by my own criteria.

Try some of these for yourself if you are having trouble in some area of your life. Where are you going? What do you want for you? Get out of the rut by going off into that almost unachievable place.

Chapter 1.18

Making It a Story

Where words fail, music speaks.

— Hans Christian Andersen

Who knows what Frank Foster had in mind when he wrote the wonderful *Blues in Hoss' Flat* or what Count Basie thought as he put together the band playing the number? It is a fine tune with lots of style, flair and pure joy. Most of us don't think much about the meaning behind the songs we hear or play, especially if they are instrumental. It is just a song.

But don't say that too loud. Music has probably been telling stories since the first cave dweller pounded in some sort of primitive time. Last year at the Big Band Camp at Shell Lake we did the *Blues in Hoss' Flat*. But first we watched this video- a classic by Jerry Lewis from his movie, *The Errand Boy*. Take a couple minutes and enjoy it.

(https://youtu.be/kS21T_p0pNA)

Lewis is, of course, pantomiming a "chairman of the board" leading a meeting. Does it help to know that the original Basie album was titled *Chairman of the*

Board? Even if it doesn't, Lewis' interpretation is a wonder to watch. I can never hear the number without this pantomime playing in my head as well.

My first real introduction to "serious" music appreciation was back in junior high (dates me, huh?) when the music teacher dropped the needle at the start of an instrumental piece. She gave us the simple instruction, "What do you hear?" No name, no introduction, just that question. Through the speaker came the opening bars of one of the great works of American music of the 20th Century, *An American in Paris*. It didn't take me long, even with my 7th grade ears, to hear a street scene, car horns and soon I saw people scurrying to and fro. After a few minutes, she stopped and asked what we heard. I don't remember what anyone else said. I'm not sure I even said anything myself. But when she told us the name and what Gershwin was doing, I was blown away.

I had heard the story in the music. I had heard what the composer was trying to tell me without having words get in the way. That one day in class 55 years ago changed my life. I don't always hear stories in the music I listen to. Sometimes I look at the name a composer gave to a song and try to put it to the music. For example, I don't know what Miles had in mind when he titled one of his numbers, *Solar*. But I hear the sun and energy, light and bright skies when I listen. But then Bruce Hornsby, Christian McBride, and Jack Dejohnette put a different arrangement of the same song on their album, *Camp Meeting*. Now the sun and light and energy are placed in a different context. I still see the power and light, but now it's in the spiritual context of a tent or camp meeting. Same notes, same basic song - but now a whole new story is being told.

Isn't that what we try to do when we play? For the next few weeks spend some quality time listening to instrumentals, stories without words, and find the stories they tell you.

Chapter 1.19

It's a Gift

Music is God's gift to man, the only art of Heaven given to earth, the only art of earth we take to Heaven.

- Walter Savage Landor (16th C. English poet)

Gifts are on our mind today. It is the day before the day before Christmas. Any last-minute gifts to buy? Any gifts I hope I get? What is a gift, though? The word comes from a word that means "give." Not a big surprise there. We know what a gift is, of course. The definitions online come as no surprise:

1. a thing given willingly to someone without payment; a present.synonyms: present, donation, offering, bestowal, bonus, award, endowment;

2. a natural ability or talent. synonyms: talent, flair, aptitude, facility, knack, bent, ability, expertise, capacity, capability, faculty; endowment, strength, genius, brilliance, skill, artistry

But the gift of heaven? Music? The only "art of heaven" that we can experience? I think I can agree with that, both as a listener and performer.

No great insights on that. Just a reminder that we as musicians at whatever stage of development we may be are gifted and givers of gifts. Be serious about your gift but enjoy it. The gift is useless if it isn't opened and used. The greatest gifts are shared.

Listen to music this week.

Make music this week.

Celebrate the "art of heaven."

Chapter 1.20

Review and Plan

Don't practice quickly and hope it gets better; practice excellence and hope it gets faster.

-Frank Campos

It is an old and trite idea to take the end of the year as a time to look back and reflect on what has been happening in one's life. But what makes something "old and trite" is that there is truth in it. Most of the time we don't stop to review and see where we have come. Why not take the end of the year as such a time?

Which is where the importance of the journal comes in. Remember a few weeks ago or so when I reminded us of the importance of keeping a journal of our practicing? Seems like busy work. But here is when you will appreciate it- and maybe get back into the habit since if you are like me you have not kept the journal for a few weeks or more.

I went back and looked at my journal from right after trumpet camp last summer. At camp we were given ideas on a regular practice routine. In addition, I was given the idea to do the Arban's exercises from page 13 - 22 and 25-28.

These are good, basic exercises that have been proven to be so fundamental it might be valuable to practice them on a regular basis.

So starting in mid-August I did that. For six weeks or so I made sure that I went through those on a regular basis. Now anyone who has played trumpet for more than a few months knows how to play these. There's nothing particularly difficult in them. For years I mostly ignored them since, well, I can play that.

But could I play them well? Could I play them at speed? Did I take the time to play them slowly enough to develop excellence? Often I would practice it quickly so I could say, "Did that. What's next?" Over these last five months I have discovered that there is an amazing depth in those exercises. They start easy; some are more difficult than others; they introduce us to key signatures and chord structures.

Last week, aware of reflection time for this week, I went back to page 13 and started playing through them. I hadn't done them all in about 2 months. I had worked on other things and had continued to notice my progression as a trumpet player. What would these sound like now?

I started with a medium tempo and found they fell into place smoothly. They moved along and felt right. Can I play them as the upper suggested tempo? Surprise. Yes, I can, at least many of them. I looked at my notes in the journal (minimal though they are) and saw that it took me a lot longer to play them in August and September because I a) couldn't play to tempo and b) missed a lot of notes.

I can talk about other reflections, but this is a good introduction to it. What I discovered was

- if I hadn't kept a journal, I would have had to rely on imperfect memory for comparison
- if I hadn't taken time for reflection I wouldn't have been as aware of my progress
- if I hadn't slowed down when first working on these back in August I wouldn't have gone beyond "just good enough"

The natural question then is "So what? What do I do with this?" As I was working through these sections of Arban's with a little better insight I discovered the ones that were still causing me difficulty. I was reminded that there are always (!!) the basics that need to be worked on. It may be "easy" to breeze through and play some of these. But there is always the opportunity to strengthen the foundation.

That brought me to the result of review and reflection- planning. I have already talked about goal-setting, etc. but that will often return as a theme. In short, for this particular review, I came up with a specific plan to refine my daily routine. I have taken the sections between pages 13 and 36, some of the very basics, and divided them into three sections. At first, I will play through each section every third day. I will be going through each section twice each week for the next 3-5 weeks. My goal- reinforce these basics and add a bit of "excellence" beyond "good enough." This will take about 10 - 15 minutes of each day's routine.

With all that aside, the biggest reflection for me is what has occurred in my trumpet playing since June when I attended the Big Band Camp at Shell Lake. The quintet I am part of then had a "peak experience" at the Vintage Band Mini Fest in Northfield, MN. I later headed back to Shell Lake for trumpet camp where my whole view of my trumpet playing took a huge positive jump. I have continued to play in two Big Bands, two concert bands and the quintet and have practiced 8 out of 10 days.

I am humbled and amazed at what has happened. I am grateful to all who helped, encouraged, challenged, instructed and allowed me to play along with you this past year.

There is more to come.

Happy New Year to all!

Chapter 1.21

Why?

Music is a language that doesn't speak in particular words. It speaks in emotions, and if it's in the bones, it's in the bones.

— Keith Richards, *According to the Rolling Stones*

In some of my surfing this past week I came across the website of Joshua MacCluer, (AKA Farley Sangels) trumpeter, educator, performance coach. One of the links was to a post he wrote titled "10 Principles for Learning Music for Beginning and Amateur Musicians." Even if many readers are past the "beginner" level, I found the list a good refresher of what we are all about as musicians. It also reminded me that even if I am not a professional musician or music educator, many times it is in the ensemble work of learning from each other that we can make a lot of progress. This blog has been for me a way to concretize my own learning and practice as a musician.

Back to the Ten Principles, though. Here are his first five principles. Comments in italics are from his explanation:

1) Start with the "Why?"

- *If we forget our real "Why?" while we are playing, we might start thinking the answer is something like, "I want to not make mistakes" or "I want to get it right" or "I want to not embarrass myself" or "I want to win this audition" or one of many ego-based desires that make music making much more difficult. Instead, we should figure out our real personal "Why?" and remind ourselves regularly, especially while we are playing music. This is very important.*

What is your real "Why?"

Several of mine- I can't stop making music. My life without it would be dull. The performance is one of the ways of sharing joy. My mind is expanded, skills developed, joy embodied. It's been happening for almost 55 years now.

2) The goal is to learn to speak music, not to learn how to play an instrument.

- *Music is a language. Therefore, like any language, the foremost goal is communication. If we want to learn how to communicate with music, it is much more important to learn what music is and how it works and how to express ourselves with it... I believe a lot of music can be more easily learned away from the instrument, or using other instruments like our ears, imagination, voices, hands, feet and bodies.*

I discovered this several years ago when I started playing in a Big Band. Almost all of my trumpet playing for decades was "concert" material- the great repertoire of wind bands. While I had listened to jazz and Big Band for just as many decades, I had little experience playing it. I found it was a whole new world. I struggled. A lot! Fortunately, I was 4th trumpet and could easily drop back (or out) when it got to the tougher parts without being missed. While I "knew" the language of jazz and big band, I couldn't "speak" it with my horn. I still had the wind band to play in and there, even with new numbers, I could drop back into a style and language I knew. It kept my chops up and helped me technically while I was learning to speak "jazz."

I am now able to do a lot more with that 4th trumpet part. Last summer at Shell Lake Big Band I learned I know the language and can even play some of the improvising. I am becoming more multi-lingual.

3) At the beginning, there are no mistakes or rules.

- *Self judgement closes down the mind and kills learning... The principle here is don't worry about mistakes. It's not about "getting it right" it's about expression. Just play and have fun, and learn quickly and easily like a child*

I have already talked about some of this in the earlier posts on The Inner Game. Suffice it to say, this is important!

4) All hail the groove! Find and feel the groove before you play.

- *The groove is where the magic lives in the music.... The first step of playing music is to connect to the groove. How to do that? Quiet your mind and try to feel it. Focus on the feeling of the music and getting that feeling into your body. You will know you have found it when your body starts to want to move with the groove.*

This can be an important part of learning the language talked about above. I know, almost instinctively, the "groove" of a Sousa march, a Holst Suite, an Alfred Reed or Samuel Hazo arrangement. I read over the piece, even if I have played it before, and my body wants to move with it. That's the groove. With jazz I have felt the groove through decades of listening. Now I am learning how to express that movement through the horn.

5) Don't worry about the notes! Make it feel right!

- *Here's a secret about music: people don't listen to music, they feel it. If a song has all the right notes but doesn't feel right, it doesn't work.... Right notes with bad rhythm are wrong notes... Victor Wooten's Rule #1, "Never lose the groove to find a note." ... If you play a wrong note with perfect rhythm, in most cases most people will not even notice. It will slide right past their ears because the feeling is right.*

Naturally this doesn't mean play whatever you want. That is the language of gibberish, the mumbling and noise of pre-language. But it does mean that it is more than just the right notes, the technically correct but lifeless string of notes. Remember in a language that the same words are available to the high school student essayist and the Pulitzer Prize-winning author. It's more than using the words, it is how and why (!) you use them. It is the passion and emotion embodied in them. Feel the music- let the feeling flow.

I am excited by these principles. They lay more of that foundation that is essential to the continuing growth of my music. I will explore more of these in the next five of these principles next week.

What are your reasons "Why?"

Note:
Thank you to Farley Sangels of Lamma Studios for permission to use The Ten Principles in this and the next chapter.
https://lammastudios.com/
He has an online course for the principles and is planning a book on them as well.

Chapter 1.22

Sing, Play, and Dance

Everything in the universe has a rhythm, everything dances.

— Maya Angelou

In the last chapter I wrote about Joshua MacCluer (Farley Sangels) and a post he wrote titled "10 Principles for Learning Music for Beginning and Amateur Musicians." Just to put this week into context, here are the first five:

1. Start with the "Why?"
2. The goal is to learn to speak music, not to learn how to play an instrument.
3. At the beginning, there are no mistakes or rules.
4. All hail the groove! Find and feel the groove before you play.
5. Don't worry about the notes! Make it feel right!

Where does he take this list? Let's follow him...

(Note: that the italicized text is from his post. The others are my thoughts.)

6) Listening is at least as important as playing.

- *We must develop the ability to listen to others and play at the same time. We must also learn what to listen to at what time. ...For example, one technique is listen to a song several times, each time listening to a different instrument or element of the music. First listen to the bass line. Then the groove. Then the feeling. Then the drums, the woodwinds, the keyboard, the violins, then the dynamics. The choices are unlimited. The most important step at the beginning is developing the ability to move our ears away from our own playing to other players or elements of the music.*

Music is meant to be heard, just like language. It is communication. What have others had to "say" in their music? Listen to it. What does Arban's 1st Characteristic Study sound like when it is played well? You will find it on You Tube. Sometimes if you are having trouble finding a groove- find a performance and listen for it. Then find it in your playing.

7) Don't practice, jam!

- *Jamming is the way to learn any language.... [T]he way to learn any language is to listen, imitate, and jam.... we don't recite speeches; we have improvised conversations. Every conversation we have with other people is an improvisation! Jamming in music is playing improvised music with other people, trying things out and learning to play with others in a way that works.... Learn to listen, reach and find new things, feel the groove together and talk about the same thing musically, in an improvised and relaxed setting.*

One of the interesting things I experienced last summer at the big band and trumpet camps was practicing with another musician. One of us would play the exercise, then the other would. It accomplished a couple of things, First it helped each of us hear the piece or exercise from the other side of the horn. We pick up nuances and phrases that way. Second, it keeps us from rushing through our practice. We pay better attention. It is only a small step from that to "jamming" together.

8) Play with other music as much as possible, even when practicing. Always keep a musical context when playing.

- *If there is no one to jam with you today, it's best to find some music to play along with. Even if you are playing your scales, having a groove to play with is very helpful. Playing with recordings or drum tracks or loops is much better than playing alone. It is also super fun and very educational to play along with recordings by great musicians of your favorite songs. Make it feel right when you play along with pros on the recording, and it will feel right when you play with people in real life.*

This goes back to the listening- and moves it further. Sure, you may do this when trying to transcribe a song, but what about just to play along with Miles Davis or the Canadian Brass? I have learned many wind band and quintet pieces that way over the years. I can feel their groove and find my place in it. And, as said above- it really is "super fun."

9) Sing!

- *The ideas we want to express [in our music] live inside of us, waiting to be expressed in the real world. However, the connection between our inner world and the outer world must be developed. The best way to do this is through singing. It removes our technical limitations and allows us to find our inner voice and ideas much more easily. Singing should be a daily practice for all musicians.... Once we know what we are hearing or trying to play, it is much easier to produce that in real life.*

I don't do it as often as I should, but singing a piece should probably be a standard of playing new or difficult pieces. Someone said at camp last summer that if you have already sung the piece, you are no longer sight-reading. Amazingly- it works. Sometimes I will sing the exercise before playing it a second time. Again, that slows me down (resting as much as playing!) and helps me get the groove a little more firmly established in my head.

10) Learn to move with the music.

- *Along with finding our voice another primary goal of music is to feel and live in the groove. The groove does not live in our heads but in our bodies. Therefore, dancing and playing drums is also very helpful. If we dance and feel the music in our bodies or maybe with a small percussion instrument, we will truly be in the flow of the musical experience and the music will flow easily and happily through us.... Dancing gets the music in our whole body, and makes for much closer connection with the musical energy. So dance! It's fun and feels great. If you're embarrassed, do it in private, and dance your way through the music you want to play. The rhythm and groove you get from that will make the instrumental playing much easier.*

Dance. Move. Let the music express itself in your body language. At a recent concert one of my friends commented on the musicians on stage. They had no energy. As you watched them you almost expected them to fall asleep mid-note. Now, there are professionals and top-notch musicians who may not move much in their performance. (Bob Dylan comes to mind, but then his musical and verbal language is so rich, he lives the movement!) Moving when practicing (or singing or listening) does make sense.

~~~~~~~~~~~~~

That groove thing keeps coming back, doesn't it? Well, after writing the first post on these 10 principles, I was doing my daily practice. After I got warmed up, etc. I pulled out one of the Concone Lyrical Studies, #7 to be exact. I have had the problem that these "lyrical" studies have not felt all that lyrical. They are a collection of notes, one after the other, on the page. In language terms, they are words strung together in a foreign language that I haven't been able to understand. I have also found it more difficult to give slow, lyrical pieces the emotion they deserve.

Well, earlier last week I found a You Tube recording of #7 and listened to it. It was okay, but it didn't move me. I did what MacCluer has talked about. I sang it, then started to play it listening and feeling for the "groove." Surprise, surprise. There really is a groove in Concone #7! The next thing I knew I was playing in that groove.

I liked it enough to play it again. I found myself moving with the music as I played it. I can't say I was dancing, but the music sure was.

This is why, at age 67, I am still a student and still learning. There is always something new in the next piece, in the middle of the old Arban's or Concone, or waiting in an unexpected phrase on the next page, around the corner of tomorrow, or even as I take a moment to pay attention to the groove of my own life and the music I make. I call this blog series reflections on life and music. If it works in the practice room, it will work in all our relationships.

- Sing.
- Play.
- Dance.

And one of my favorite all time quotes:

Those who dance were thought to be insane
by those who could not hear the music.

Note:
Thank you to Farley Sangels of Lamma Studios for permission to use The Ten Principles in this and the previous chapter.
https://lammastudios.com/
He has an online course for the principles and is planning a book on them as well.

Chapter 1.23

Be Crazy- Crazy Good

Those who dance were thought to be insane by those who could not hear the music.

I know- I ended the previous post with that same quote. Well, consider it the theme, the phrase that ties last week to this week. It is a segue into what is like a coda to last week. For when I was finished typing it for last week, I could hear the unmistakable voice of camp director, Mr. Baca:

Are you crazy?

and the response, as always

Yeah- **crazy good!**

Not sure what to say about that I Googled the phrase "crazy good" and ended up at the online Urban Dictionary where I found:

a. Awesome, amazing, cool, stunning, super cool

Knowing the humility for which we trumpet players are so well known (?), that made sense. Hey- this is about being "crazy good." Awesome, amazing, etc. It is beyond just plain good. Man, it's crazy good!

But that's not what the quote is about. It's more than being especially good, talented or stunning. And sure enough, right after that first definition was another:

> b. The feelings following an enlightenment; typically in creative work (elevation of work of art, idea, ability, level of happiness), where one is playing with and extending further. As the paradigm has shifted, others may express the genuine feeling you have actually gone crazy, however the opposite could be true and the path to awesomeness is being cemented.

Wow. Now that I have had happen. A moment of enlightenment, that old "Aha!" moment, leads down a path that you had never thought you would be following. The idea or ability or level of happiness is beyond what we have thought to be "normal." And that can feel like crazy!

Isn't that what musicians are looking to do- go beyond the "normal," find the new idea, the new experience, even in the song you have played hundreds or more times? You finish playing that exercise in Clarke or the Etude in Concone and you find yourself sitting in silence. Something has just happened. You can't explain it, but you know it is real. People may look at those hours of practicing studies from the 19th Century and look at you and say,

What? Are you crazy?

and you smile and say,

Yeah- **Crazy good!**

Or you are sick and tired of that piece your band plays every gig. There isn't even a place of solos or improvising. Sure, the group plays it well. You should after how many times you have played it. But then there's that moment when the audience stands and applauds and you realize you have just played it in a way that you never remember before. Sure, same notes, same rhythms. But the groove? The expression? The tightness of the group? You smile to yourself and say,

Yeah- Crazy good.

Or there's that memory of that place on the west facing lookout at the park. There's room for maybe 20 or 30 people- and the place is full. It is almost sunset on a perfect day. People are chatting and discussing everything from the weather to politics to how to keep the kids quiet long enough for you to see the sun set.

You didn't need to worry. As the sun sinks into the western horizon and the colors begin to grow and deepen, the crowd speaks more softly. Even the children are entranced by this every day event as daylight lessens and shadows lengthen. You realize that the whole group is now silent. Adults and children in awe of one of the most common events on the planet. In awe as if there has never been one like it- and never will be again.

Try to explain that to someone who may not be able to get it, who doesn't hear the music of the sun or the birds in the forest behind you. Try to describe what it means to one of those overly logical-types who want answers.

What? Are you crazy or something?
Yeah- **crazy good!**

I have written about the language of music and the ability to speak it, live it, understand it, play it. It is a wordless language that makes no sense to someone who has never experienced it. It is tough enough for most of us on those days when the lip won't stay on the right note, the brain forgets how to play a "G major" scale, and you run out of breath half-way through every phrase.

But we keep coming back because we know the language and we know it works. Not every time, not every day, but when it happens, we are transformed.

So, I will end by again quoting Mr. Baca:

Let's get crazy!
Crazy good!

Chapter 1.24

Observe and Imitate

Try to find the best teachers, listen to the finest playing, and try to emulate that. Be true to the music.

- Wynton Marsalis

I have been reading *Words Without Music*, an interesting memoir/autobiography by modern American composer Philip Glass. It is a good insight into the creative process of one remarkable composer and how he developed into the person he has become. Reading it with an eye to seeing creativity develop is worth the time. At one point he is describing his working with sculptor Richard Serra. Glass spent several years working with Serra as a "day-job" to support his composing. He expressed to Serra one day that he would like to learn how to draw to which Serra replied that he could do that by teaching Glass how to "see" and then he would be able to draw.

That was an eye-opening insight for Glass. He reports the following thought that flowed from it:

Drawing is about seeing, dancing is about moving, writing (narrative and especially poetry) is about speaking, and music is about hearing. I next realized that music training was absolutely about *learning to hear* - going completely past everyday listening. p. 223 [emphasis added]

This reminded me of an article about Clark Terry on the Jazz Advice website. (http://www.jazzadvice.com/clark-terrys-3-steps-to-learning-improvisation/) Terry's three steps to improvising are:

Imitation, Assimilation, Innovation.

That simple. (Yeah. Right!) Terry define's *imitation* this way:

Listening. Learning lines by ear. Transcribing solos. Absorbing a player's feel, articulation, and time.

The same as Glass's insight- learning to hear. Paying attention.

We've all heard someone say (or have said it ourselves) that they just don't "get" or "understand" that music. The first time you hear music from a completely different culture based on scales and rhythm that is "foreign" to us, we scratch our heads in wonder. What that means on some level is that we are not listening or able to listen to the music as it is meant to be heard. Our own brains don't expect it to sound that way.

Learning to hear. Paying attention.

But we can keep working at it. We can keep listening. We can train ourselves to listen differently. Too often we expect things to be just like they have been before. Or in a way that we are used to. Glass himself faced a great deal of criticism and even hatred for the type of "odd" music he was writing. When he started in the 50s and 60s "modern music" was considered the music of the 1900s- 1920s or so. People came on stage and attempted to stop his concerts! They weren't able to hear- and therefore made a judgement about its quality and even its definition as music.

I would go beyond listening to learn to improvise. I think it is essential to being a musician of any type of music. Hearing what it sounds like; hearing what it feels like. Then picking up our instrument and trying to imitate it. The more we listen, the more we are open to hearing, the greater our musical skill will become and the deeper our understanding of music will go.

What this boils down to is going beyond the music theory and an intellectual understanding. The website Brain Pickings (https://www.brainpickings.org/2012/04/12/elliott-schwartz-music-ways-of-listening/) has a post from the 1982 book by author and composer Elliot Schwartz *Music: Ways of Listening*. The book outlines seven essential skills of learning to listen in this age where, he believes, we have been "dulled by our built-in twentieth-century habit of tuning out."

The first skill is:

- Develop your sensitivity to music. Try to respond esthetically to all sounds, from the hum of the refrigerator motor or the paddling of oars on a lake, to the tones of a cello or muted trumpet. When we really hear sounds, we may find them all quite expressive, magical and even 'beautiful.' On a more complex level, try to relate sounds to each other in patterns: the successive notes in a melody, or the interrelationships between an ice cream truck jingle and nearby children's games.

It's all about hearing. The other six skills Schwartz explains help us guide our learning and our hearing, going deeper and broader.

- *Time* is a crucial component of the musical experience. Develop a sense of time as it passes: duration, motion, and the placement of events within a time frame.
- Develop a *musical memory*. While listening to a piece, try to recall familiar patterns, relating new events to past ones and placing them all within a durational frame.
- If we want to read, write or talk about music, we must acquire a working *vocabulary*.
- Try to develop *musical concentration*, especially when listening to lengthy pieces.

- Try to listen *objectively and dispassionately*. Concentrate upon 'what's there,' and not what you hope or wish would be there.
- Bring *experience and knowledge* to the listening situation. That includes not only your concentration and growing vocabulary, but information about the music itself: its composer, history and social context. Such knowledge makes the experience of listening that much more enjoyable.

This isn't just about music, of course. The relation to writing, or cooking, or being good at your job can be easily made. From the Brain Pickings post:

Perhaps most interestingly, you can substitute "reading" for "listening" and "writing" for "music," and the list would be just as valuable and insightful, and just as needed an antidote to the dulling of our modern modes of information consumption.

Go for it. Listen!

Then, really hear.

Then imitate.

Chapter 1.25

Assimilate- Practice!

We are what we repeatedly do. Excellence, then, is not an act, but a habit.

—Aristotle

In the last post I mentioned Clark Terry's three important bits of learning to improvise: *Imitate, Assimilate, Innovate.* These are also important in growing as a musician in any genre, even if we never have to improvise.

I discussed listening as basic to imitating. In our listening we pick up on things that are going on in the music we are listening to. We pay attention to what is going on within the music and even within our own emotions and responses to the music. Imitation, in Clark Terry's thought, is *learning by ear* and then *absorbing the feel, articulation and time* of whatever you are listening to.

Well, in that absorption something else begins to happen- the second of Clark Terry's bits:

Assimilate.

I looked up the general definition of assimilate before digging into what he meant by it. Here is a little from the Free Dictionary online:

Assimilate means:

1. to learn (information, a procedure, etc.) and understand it thoroughly
2. to become absorbed, incorporated, or learned and understood
3. to bring or come into harmony; adjust or become adjusted to
4. to become or cause to become similar

To *learn and understand thoroughly,* in the case of musical listening is not just saying, "Oh, I get the theory behind what is being played!" It goes beyond understanding what is happening. It is hearing the theory applied. It moves from getting the theory to hearing, feeling, catching hold of what the theory sounds, feels, and perhaps even looks like.

Assimilation then moves to allowing what *we learn and understand thoroughly* to become *absorbed and incorporated* in what we are doing. Remember, we are imitating Clark Terry, Miles, Coltrane, or Herb Alpert. Imitation is beyond aping or mimicking- it is absorbing the style so it becomes yours. As a result, we ourselves can move into *harmony, become adjusted* to whatever it is we are listening to and imitating. That is an important step that cannot be overlooked, or short changed.

On the Jazz Advice website ([http://www.jazzadvice.com/clark-ter-rys-3-steps-to-learning-improvisation/](http://www.jazzadvice.com/clark-terrys-3-steps-to-learning-improvisation/)) where they talked about these three things of Clark Terry's they described some of this step this way:

> Assimilation means ingraining these stylistic nuances, harmonic devices, and lines that you've transcribed into your musical conception… truly connecting them to your ear and body. This is where the hours of dedication and work come in.
>
> • Get into the practice room and repeat these lines over and over again, hundreds of times, until they are an unconscious part of your musical conception.
>
> • Take these phrases through all keys, all ranges, and all inversions.
>
> • Begin slowly and incrementally increase the speed until you can easily play them.
>
> • Don't feel satisfied until you can play these lines in your sleep.
>
> This is not an easy step to complete.

Yeah- I know.

So what now?

You are what you practice most.

-Richard Carlson

Well, the basic answer is "Go and do it." That phrase, *connecting them to your ear and body*, is really the goal. But can I really do that? Do I have the motivation to do what needs to be done to become a better trumpet player? What about those days when that trumpet looks like it weighs a ton and the mouthpiece seems to have all kinds of nails sticking out before I even pick up the horn?

At this stage of the learning, we are working at being similar in our style to whatever we are listening to. We just have to keep at it. Maybe we are working on a difficult passage in a classical wind band piece. The notes run by too fast. Keep playing it. Build it up in your head. Listen to a recording of it. (Much gratitude to YouTube on this one!) I have been doing that with that first characteristic study from Arban's book. I found a recording by Paul Mayes of it at full speed and listen time after time to it. (https://www.youtube.com/watch?v=PgGyqddyFK0) What are the nuances? I watch his fingering and see if he uses any alternates. I even watch how he moves the trumpet on his lips. It is the whole process of imitating- hearing, feeling, seeing.

Don't overlook singing the music as well. Part of the assimilation is to get it into your head. Sing it. Then sing it again. Get the feel. I can usually sing something closer to the full tempo sooner than I can play it. But they work together.

These tricks work. They help me pay attention to the music and how I feel as I'm playing. But more than that, they also introduce me to a way of playing that I may not have known before. When I try to improvise, for example, I tend to be more melodic, Miles Davis in "Birth of the Cool"-era or even Al Hirt in "Java." I have not been able to think fast enough to do some of the bebop licks. But I have been listening to them and even singing some of them.

What I continue to be amazed at is that this is all taking place for me now- 55 years after I first learned the trumpet. It is possible- and exciting- for an old dog to learn new tricks. Some of it is common sense. Some of it is just the old line- practice, practice, practice. What do I want to become as a musician? Well practice that.

And usually all it takes is to pick up the horn and start those long tones and my mind and body begin to come together. It's about the music.

Chapter 1.26

Innovate

Without deviation from the norm, progress is not possible.

— Frank Zappa

As you may have noticed most of these posts have been summaries of things I have discovered in my "research" of practice and performance, added to some basic common sense and then bundled in a motivational style. I am writing out of discovery mode and trying to learn things myself as well as share some insights with you. I am not pretending to be an expert on any of this. I am a learner on a new journey using this as a way to put into words what I am finding and inviting you on the journey with me.

This one is a good example of how I am working on figuring out many things about being a trumpet player. Over the past two weeks I talked about the first two of what Clark Terry has called the three essentials of learning to improvise- *imitate, assimilate*, and *innovate*. I have said that even without being a jazz improviser, these are essentials to being better musicians and having a more interesting life.

We start by listening- a lot- so that we can imitate what we hear. What better way to learn than to listen to and imitate the great masters? Then we allow what we have heard and worked on to become a part of us- it is assimilated into who we are and into our music.

All that, for me, is the easy part. I can listen, I can work hard at imitating, I can internalize some of the great music I want to play. It is how I have been able to play some of the solos in concert band or my Basin Street Blues solo in big band. It is how I have succeeded at some of the pieces in the quintet where I have a unique part. I can do that!

But this innovation thing? I'm not so sure about that.

So I go back to the Jazz Advice (http://www.jazzadvice.com/clark-ter-rys-3-steps-to-learning-improvisation/) website where they say this about Clark Terry's third essential- *innovation*.

> [It is] creating a fresh and personal approach to the music.... [and] is the direct result of hours upon hours of imitation and assimilation. Take a look at the great innovators that this music has already seen. Each one spent countless hours studying harmony, solos, form, tunes, etc. In order to realize their own personal concept.

We all know what that means and how it has played out over the years. We know that Miles had a different style from Chet Baker, even in the "cool jazz" era. We know that Beethoven had a different sound than Brahms. We know that the New York Symphony plays differently from the Chicago Symphony. That, I know, is the result of innovation. Or to put it as bluntly as Frank Zappa- they all deviated from the norm- and music progress occurred.

Innovation in trumpet playing is finding your own style. Very, very few of us will ever be Miles or Maynard, Baker or Alpert. They all have changed the sound of contemporary music- and in very different ways.

Innovation starts for us in the practice room when we take one of those Arban studies and change the articulation. Maybe we move slurring around or change dynamics. What feels good to you? What feels like an expression of your music? Pull out a fake book or one of Aebersold's books and just work on different ways of playing the "head." Don't do any improvising yet. Experiment with tone and tempo; emphasize the notes and phrases in different ways. Sing it first. Then play it.

On Herb Alpert's most recent album he takes the classic "Take the 'A' Train" in 3/4 time. Innovation.

"Yes, but..." is the thought that comes to my mind. *"I've tried it,"* I respond to myself, *"and it sounds pretty poor. I don't think fast enough, I don't know enough music theory, on and on...."*

Remember the Inner Game? That's good, old Self One sitting there on my shoulder bringing me down. He won't allow me to even try. For one, it is too much like work and, for another, can take too much time. Yeah, so? Do I want this? I know I'm not going to make some big musical revolution happen, but it will be inside me. It will have an impact on the bands and groups I play with as we work together to make music interesting.

I said at the beginning of this post that these are "motivational-style" posts aimed at much at myself as for you. That means I will have to do something about these. I will have to take my own suggestions and try them on some consistent basis. *"Yeah, I tried it, but it didn't go well"* just can't cut it. There's a Big Band camp coming in June, not to mention the quintet doing some gigs and new pieces for us. If I always play the way I have always played, I will never change and never improve.

Let me know what you have found as ways to innovate your playing and musicality.

Again from the Jazz Advice post:

> The steps of imitation, assimilation, and innovation are not limited to "jazz" music. Take any style or concept that resonates with you and incorporate it into your playing through this process. You may like the harmonies of Ravel or the rhythms found in traditional Indian music. Listen to them, figure them out, analyze them, practice them, and finally use them in new and innovative ways in your improvisations. (http://www.jazzadvice.com/clark-terrys-3-steps-to-learning-improvisation/)

Chapter 1.27

Using Energy

Music has always been a matter of Energy to me, a question of Fuel. Sentimental people call it Inspiration, but what they really mean is Fuel.

-Hunter S. Thompson

Energy.

(Excuse me for a digression into physics.)

What IS energy?

Actually "energy" can be defined as a number of different types of energy.

- *Kinetic* energy of a moving object,
- *Potential* energy stored by an object's position
- *Elastic* energy stored by stretching solid objects,
- *Chemical* energy released when a fuel burns,
- *Radiant* energy carried by light, and
- *Thermal* energy due to an object's temperature.

An important bit of knowledge about energy:

- All forms of energy are convertible to other kinds of energy;
- energy can be neither created nor be destroyed;
- it can change from one form to another.

Why all this about energy? Well, it started when I came across a note from the camp last summer that said we should always play with the same amount of energy. It shouldn't matter if we are playing the "1812 Overture" or "Mary Had a Little Lamb." The energy needs to be the same. A soft and gentle passage needs as much energy as the loud ones we trumpets are known to love. A slow, prayerful piece has to come across to the listener with the same amount of fullness as a Sousa march.

I know that on one level that sounds like a dream, something that is almost an oxymoron. How can one have quiet energy or powerful softness? Then I noticed a You Tube video of the Canadian Brass doing their wonderful arrangement of Amazing Grace, a trumpet feature. As I watched the lead trumpet, I realized that I couldn't tell by looking whether he was in high or low register. I turned off the sound and watched. He played with the same ease- and energy- whether he was loud, soft, low, or high. Which is why the piece is so powerful.

Energy is not about pressure or loudness. It is about the underlying power. Reading the list of types of energy shows that there is a lot of energy in an object just sitting there. But if that object is a car, its energy changes significantly when traveling down the road at 80 mph.

Let's take that nice, concert F, our G. When we were just starting to play, we couldn't play it loudly or softly with equal presence. When we went too soft- pianissimo, it kind of went flat and lost its sound quality- its energy. When we tried to play it loud- fortissimo- it cracked and splattered. We really hadn't learned how to master energy.

As we have moved through our learning curves on playing, we have discovered that we can play pianissimo without losing quality and fortissimo without splattering. This is an essential part of our improvement as musicians. It is a lot of work to get to that point. Every group or band I have ever played in has had that same problem. We have greater difficulty maintaining energy on slow or soft pieces. We have greater trouble holding a note's sound when it's a slow half of whole note in a passage. Or what about coming in on a pianissimo high note?

Several things come to mind about that. First is what Mr. Baca talked about when he did a master class or session with us at camp. Perhaps it is best described in this quote from Don Jacoby:

> *We never blow to the horn.*
> *We blow through the horn.*
> *We never blow up to a note,*
> *we blow out to it.*

When I took the lead pipe off my horn and just played through it, I discovered the energy in the note even though there was no note as I was used to hearing. Remember that energy and play with the lead pipe back. Go up the scale and play each note with the same energy.

Which is the second thing about this energy discussion- support. The support of the sound, the note is part of the energy. Look at the list above. The support is the potential energy of the note and the elastic energy of the expanding and contracting diaphragm. It is there with the kinetic energy of the air moving between our lips into the mouthpiece and through the horn.

The reason this works is the third thing I realized- energy is neither created or destroyed. It always is there; it is just transformed. With our music, we are transforming the energy from all these sources into sound energy (not listed above). It's all energy. Therefore, the better or more controlled and utilized our energy is, the better the sound.

Which brings me back to the same old line:

- Practice, practice, practice

But not just playing, being deliberate in our playing. Take time to play those long tones. That was a real revelation for me. When I started doing that in a regular, intentional way, my sound improved almost immediately. I was learning how to control, utilize, the energy more efficiently. I was building support in my lungs, diaphragm, and embouchure so that the sound can be maintained.

In one of the Jazz Academy videos on You Tube, Marcus Printup of the Jazz at Lincoln Center Orchestra, suggests doing a whole series of soft, triple-p, concert Fs as long tones. The result is learning how to maintain energy. It gets us listening to the sound more carefully. We experience what energy feels like as we make the sound.

As always, we need to be intentional about what we are doing. Even if you don't have a detailed plan (and I never do, hence I will not say you should, even though I probably should!) have a series of intentionally developed routines that allow for the energy to be channeled into music. We discover our own sources of energy and how to utilize them for the benefit of our playing.

By the way, I think this is one of the reasons why most practice instructions say to quite before you get tired. If we have lost your energy, the music we are playing won't have as much and we will learn incorrectly. To rest, to take a break and recharge our energy is important. We will get more endurance as we continue, but over doing it on one day and then having to recuperate isn't helpful.

As always, I will add, that this is all
just like the rest of life.

Chapter 1.28

Your Story

Music is philosophy. Every chord, every word tells a story. If you listen you will know its meaning.

> -Kamanda Ndama (African Musician, Philosopher, Poet and Songwriter)

Composer, arranger, and educator Stanley Curtis has a post on his blog Trumpet Journey (https://www.trumpetjourney.com/2015/09/28/happy-birthday-and-the-importance-of-story-song-and-support/) that talks about the three "S"s, the three key elements he believes all great trumpet players have. They are simply

- Story
- Song and
- Support

As to the first, *Story*, Curtis writes:

Each of us has a unique story. That story may be an actual account of some event, or even the story of our life. But we also have our own stories that we keep coming back to, such as "beauty is great," or "old things are cool" or "technology is what I'm about." These are our thematic points that our choices point to.

Some might say that part of the "story" is your own personal mission statement, your view of what it is you see as your life's mission. That is your guiding principle. Most of us never think much about that, but we all live our personal "Theme and Variations" in what we do and how we go about our lives.

Most of us are more than familiar with the Arban's "Variations on *Carnival of Venice*." There's an introduction, the theme and then the incredible variations. Another similar composition is Charles Ives' "Variations on *America*". Throughout each composition the basic theme repeats, of course, but all kinds of styles and flourishes are added. For the listener the goal is to see the connections with the original theme. For the performer and/or composer it is to make those connections real and interesting without going so far afield that the original concept is lost.

That's the "story" we each continue to "riff" on as we go through our lives. Sometimes the riff is fast and furious, putting as much energy as we can into it. Other times it slows down and floats along with ease. Then it switches to a minor key or some odd set of tonalities. Yet, underneath it, is "you", your theme. As Curtis says above this "theme" or "story" is what informs the choices and that these choices support.

He goes on:

> Choices about repertoire, style, equipment, venues, and even the clothes we wear when we perform can help create our own story and the story that each generation needs to hear. Many players perform to a story that is going on inside their heads. As listeners, we can sense that something dramatic is happening.

Choices. We all make them all the time. Most of the time we don't even think about them. Most of the time the choices we make fall into the pattern of our story. It's who we are. Why did we choose to play trumpet, instead of any of the other instruments? How does "being a trumpet player" fit into my view of my story? Why did I continue to play the trumpet? Many people learn to play instruments but many quit after college, if not before.

Last year at trumpet camp there were those who are planning on making music their career, while others will have other professions. Yet there is something about the trumpet that obviously fits our individual stories. Why?

That's the choice. It helps define us. It fills a place in our lives that nothing else quite does. How then do we tell that story in our music?

Think about your story. What is it? Where do you want to go? How does music help you do that? How does that come out in your music? Spend some time reflecting on that and practice *your* story this week.

-Link for above quotes from Trumpet Journey (https://www.trumpetjourney.com/2015/09/28/happy-birthday-and-the-importance-of-story-song-and-support/)

Chapter 1.29

Your Song

Most people die with their music still locked up inside them.

— Benjamin Disraeli

The previous post was on "Story," the first of three things that composer, arranger, and educator Stanley Curtis on his blog Trumpet Journey (https://www.trumpetjourney.com/2015/09/28/happy-birthday-and-the-importance-of-story-song-and-support/) calls the three "S"s. These are what he sees as the three key elements all great trumpet players have in common. They are simply

- Story
- Song and
- Support

Let's look at the second thing- **Song**!

Curtis wrote:

This is how we play what we play. This song can be sung with heart-on-the-sleeve romanticism, laser-beam clarity, or rhetorical interpretation. This is our personal song we sing on the trumpet when we play. Each of our voices are different–and they should be. Our song is the meeting place of our phrasing, our interpretation, our experience and, of course, our tone. I learned a beautiful lesson about tone from a former colleague of mine, the great euphonium player named Roger Behrend. He said it helps him to think about tone in terms of color, texture and taste. So, for instance, if you are thinking about maroon, velvet and chocolate, you get an especially luxurious sound. Or, perhaps you're thinking golden, rough and with the taste of jambalaya, like I do, when I hear [Louis Armstrong]...

How we play what we play.

Just starting with that idea is enough to put it into a framework. Miles Davis famously said:

You hear three notes and you know it's Herb Alpert.

While some argue about the possible meaning, there is enough circumstantial evidence to indicate this was not a condemnation of Alpert. Instead, it is a way of saying that Herb knew (and still knows) what his song is. One could certainly say the same about Davis or Chet Baker or Louis Armstrong. In every performance, in every recording, you can, in one way or another, hear the underlying song of the musician.

No- that does not mean that all the songs they do sound alike. Far from it. It's the jambalaya Curtis mentions in Armstrong. It's the California Cool in Chet Baker. It's a life of daring and innovation driving Davis. It is a curious and profound spirituality in Coltrane. It's how they play.

The song we sing on the trumpet when we play

The song is your story. The song, as you play it, tells who you are. Now, I don't want to make too much of this. It isn't all that evident in those of us who aren't full-time professionals. Or maybe it is. Think about your playing. Think about how you play. Most of us have our "style" regardless of the music. Pay attention to it. is it you? Have fun with it in your practice room. You will notice yourself being more consistent.

The meeting place of our

- phrasing
- interpretation
- experience
- tone

That's really the crux of it.

What about me? What is my song? How do I play what I play? I never thought of that until reading Curtis' post. But then again, I knew it in my intuitive self. It started- and continues today, 55 years later- with one song- "When the Saints Go Marching In". I can now play that in all 12 major keys! (Some keys way more slowly than others!) I have at least 50 various versions of the song in my iTunes library from Dixieland to Bluegrass to "classical." Closely related to it is "Amazing Grace." I have around 90 variations of that song. Throw in "Tijuana Taxi/Spanish Flea" for some color and you can hear my song. It's how I play what I play.

What I have is blues and jazz, American gospel, a sense of gratitude, and joy. I wrap that into everything I play. It is not a surprise that the only song I have a solo on in either big band is "Basin Street Blues." My favorite solo piece for concert band is the (for me) blues-driven "Song Without Words" from Holst's *2nd Military Suite*. I can probably hear that in my style from time to time when playing a Bach chorale, Moravian hymn, or Gabrieli's "Canzon #2."

So what? Always an important question. What difference does it make if I know this or not?

Does my song change? Do I play a different song today than I did 55 years ago, or even 10 years ago? For me, no. But the song does find different interpretations, tone, phrasing- all based on the changing of my experiences. Remember, the "song" is the meeting place of all those things. It is how the story gets told.

It is yours!

Don't lose it- and don't let it stay locked up inside you.

Chapter 1.30

Your Support

Flatter me, and I may not believe you. Criticize me, and I may not like you. Ignore me, and I may not forgive you. Encourage me, and I may not forget you.

-William Arthur

The past two posts were on "Story" and "Song", the first two of three things that composer, arranger, and educator Stanley Curtis on his blog Trumpet Journey calls the three "S"s. (https://www.trumpetjourney.com/2015/09/28/happy-birthday-and-the-importance-of-story-song-and-support/) These are what he sees as the three key elements all great trumpet players have in common. They are simply

- Story
- Song and
- Support

Let's look at the third- **Support!**

Curtis wrote:

> But to keep the song going, which keeps the story fresh, we all need the support of our technique, our fundamentals, our use of air, and our "chops." For most of us, this comes down to consistent, mindful practice over many years. We are also looking for the right equipment to help us get there. Equipment and practice routines seem to be the subjects of most the trumpet chatter out there on the web and in studios. We all want to be able to play better, faster and higher. I know I do. But I think we all understand the limitations of mouthpieces, technique and high notes without a great singing style. Or without a musical story to tell. Let's let support be what it is: help for a greater cause.

As I read Curtis' thoughts, I realized that this is a good summary of much of what we have been talking about on this blog since the beginning.

- Technique
- Fundamentals
- Consistent mindful practice

He also points out that without the song and the story, even the best equipment is just about mechanical things based on physics. Music is just sound vibrations hitting people's eardrums unless there's a story and a song.

That also brings us back to one of the "fundamentals" for many of us, lessons. They can be formal with a specific teacher with specific assignments and schedule. They can also be "informal" ranging from asking a fellow trumpet player to listen and evaluate what you are doing to sitting in with a group and jamming. What is important is to get the opinion of others. As I have said before I have had several such people in my trumpet playing life recently and the change has been dramatic (from my point of view, anyway.)

What can we see new today, then. In general support can be defined as:

1. give assistance to;

2. enable to function or act;

3. give approval, comfort, or encouragement to;

4. prod, spur, egg on, goad, provoke.

Here are some questions and thoughts that came to mind as I looked at that list:

- What (or who) can give you assistance in telling your story through your trumpet playing?

    There are the obvious answers- consistent practice, developing mindfulness and all the techniques that go along with that. But you are in your own unique place. What can give that to you? What resources are there around you.

    When I realized I wanted (and needed) to do more with learning jazz improvisation I remembered that there is a jazz jam every month in town here. I contacted the two people who organize it and asked them for some time. We haven't scheduled it yet. I'm going to send them a note when I get done with this. I have also been working on my scales which I have been told is an essential for improvisation.

- What can enable you to function or act in a way that improves your ability to play your song?

    Again, beyond the standard answers- what might you do to improve your method of practicing? Ask someone what they do. Spend some time surfing the Internet, Googling as specific as you can. I became aware that I was not working on flexibility as much as I may need to. I simply searched on trumpet flexibility exercises. I had more than I needed. I spent some time comparing them and found that most were similar if not exactly the same. I had my basic flexibility.

- What is the needed balance in your life between positive criticism and encouragement?

- None of us will improve if all we ever get is praise. Find the teacher, friend, musician who can give you constructive criticism as well as be able to tell you what you are doing right. I recently sent my teacher a link to some of the performances of the quintet I play in, asking for

feedback. He started right out with encouragement- a positive statement. He then promised to spend some time at our next lesson going
over the videos with me with a critically supportive ear. I am looking
forward to it.

- How do you find the people, places, situations that can prod and spur
  you, egg you on to greater width and depth in your music?

- This one follows on the previous one. Don't be afraid of finding new
  situations. I volunteered to take a solo in the one big band the other
  night. With all the songs we have I may never get the chance to play it
  in a performance- but hey, you never know. Now I have to work on it!

This IS what life is all about with music, work, or friendship. We sum it
up, all of it, in the word support. We too often believe we need to be rugged
individualists, able to take care of ourselves no matter what. That's a dangerous
bunch of baloney! Musicians know that- we play in groups from duets to concert bands. Sure, we solo, but we would get as bored with it as our audiences if
that was all we did.

Be open to the support you need. Be honest with yourself. Then go get your
support- YOUR team.

Chapter 1.31

Sing Your Song

If you cannot teach me to fly, teach me to sing.

— J.M. Barrie, author of Peter Pan

After a previous post I got this from my friend and fellow trumpet player, Steve:

> I began to think about the human voice either spoken or sung and I thought about the trumpet voice. I remember being taught that if one could make a good sound on the mouth piece, that sound would be even better on the trumpet itself.

This directed me toward a number of things related to music, voice, and trumpet.

- The human voice itself is an incredible musical instrument. - Scat singing in jazz is an excellent example. Some of Bob Dylan's greatest lyrics make no "logical" sense but are an incredible melding of the melody and the human voice singing actual words. The words form the melody as much as the notes. It does take a whole orchestra to match the range and wonder of the human voice.

- Instrumental music often is asked to imitate the human voice. - One could ask whose vocal style should it be imitating? Most composers are thinking lyrical music at that point, but I can imagine an instrumental sound like say folksinger John Prine's gravelly style, the rough edge of John Fogerty, or the smooth as velvet with rough feel of Jim Morrison of the Doors. Cantabile- In a smooth singing style

- Many teachers suggest singing the part first before even picking up the horn. - One said that means when you are playing it on the horn, you really aren't sight-reading it for the first time.

But even beyond the connections of voice and instrumental music Steve points us trumpet players to the trumpet voice itself and our using it in the best, most effective, and most musical way possible. Steve mentioned that if you can make a "good" sound on just the mouthpiece, the horn will only enhance it. Borrowing a technique I discovered last summer, let me add a bit to that.

Pull the tuning slide out and just play the lead pipe. Make it a solid, centered sound. Listen and keep it centered. THAT, my instructors have been telling me, is the basic on which all notes on the trumpet are based. The simple act of a solid, centered sound. The recommendation is to do that every day as a start to your playing. Get that in your mind and you have the solid voice of your trumpet and trumpet playing. That brief action on Mr. Baca's part at the Big Band camp literally began a major transformation in my trumpet playing.

It isn't even about the "buzz". It's about the movement of air. It's not about being in tune with some external standard. It is about the specific, centered, focused sound of the unique horn you are playing. All music is the movement of air. It is air vibrating at specific wavelengths. I was reminded of this just this past Sunday when I attended a concert and clinic put on by the Compass Rose Brass from Minneapolis. The trumpet clinic reminded us of this. It is one of those simple foundations of trumpet playing that we often forget. Keep the air moving at that steady pace. Learn how to move the air as needed. It isn't even all about the embouchure, although that is involved. It is about the air.

That in itself is enough to think about when talking about the voice of the trumpet- singing the song through the instrument. It is allowing the sound of the horn, the sound of the air, and the sound in your head to become music.

Which leads to *your* voice. We have talked about that from the outside when talking about story and song in the past month. But you and I may both have the same song and come from the same place, but our voice will be different. Like those singers mentioned above. No two have the same voice. Or take a song like Dylan's "Mr. Tambourine Man". A beautiful, mystical, mysterious song- when Dylan sings it. A beautiful "pop" song when even such a talented group as The Byrds sing it.

Even if you are not a good singer, you still sing through your instrument. Think about that a second. My horn becomes an extension of my voice; it is how I can sing. The Compass Rose clinic on Sunday reminded me that we need to think about the song we are playing, not just playing the notes. Think about the meaning of the music; translate that meaning into the way you play the notes; it's your voice, let it sing.

Chapter 1.32

Practice and Performance

Be harder on yourself in the practice room and be easier on yourself in performance.

-Bryan Edgett

Going through my notes from the end of last year's Trumpet Camp at Shell Lake, I came across this note:

Practice like you want to perform; perform like you practice

I had some kind of intuitive idea of what that meant, kind of along the lines of the quote above from trumpeter and professor Bryan Edgett. Practice is where you work out what you want to do and performance is where you share it with others. It also meant to me that when I am practicing, I should NOT just be playing the notes on the page. I need to be digging into all the aspects of the music- tempo, tone, shape, groove, etc. If I can't find those in the practice room, they won't be there when I go to perform them.

I have seen that happen in my own playing with a concert band. I practice my part and have it down cold. Technically it feels right and I'm feeling good about myself. Then I get to the next rehearsal and I hear my part with the rest of the band and, oops, I can't make it happen. That means that on some level my practice has been missing some things. One of those is to see practice as a performance.

So I dropped an email to one of the faculty from last summer's camp, Bill Bergren. I asked him what he took that statement about practicing and perform-ing to mean. Here's his answer:

> Performing at a high level is a habit. Develop that habit by practicing at a high level. This most often means:
> - Fundamentals make up 50% to 75% of your daily practice.
> - Slow down to the point where you can play without mistakes.
> - Repetition is your friend.

I told Bill that I would riff on what he said- and he gave me lots of things to think about. Let's start at the top.

I had never thought of high level performing as a "habit." Sure, I knew about muscle memory and getting in the habit of doing things the right way so I don't have to fix them later. But to see performing itself as a habit was an expanded insight. If I have not gotten into the habit of practicing at a high level, I won't be able to do any performing well.

About the same time Bill wrote me the above, we had a brief conversation online about the meme that Malcolm Gladwell wrote about in his 2008 book, *Outliers*. What has come to be called the "10,000 Hour Rule" basically says that the key to becoming expert in any field is to have put in 10,000 hours of practice. In our instant gratification society this came as a shock to some. You mean I can't be an expert at this for what, 3 1/2 years of 8-hour days? Sorry, not for me.

The other side of instant gratification is finding an "easy" answer to getting what I want. So, if I sit down and play for x amount of time for x number of days, even if it is 3 1/2 years, I will be an expert. Let's get started. Well, that naturally doesn't happen that way since someone with that type of attitude isn't going to stick with it for 3 1/2 months let alone 3 1/2 years because they will not see themselves changing.

That's because just practicing for 10,000 hours alone isn't going to do it. If you do it wrong for those 10,000 hours, you will be an expert at doing it wrong. If you settle for less than your best for those 3 1/2 years, you will be great at being less than your best. Hence, Bill's comment above that the practicing at a high level is what it's about.

But 10,000 hours of practicing and performing at a high level will lead to even higher levels of practicing and performing. THAT I find exciting and motivating. That does mean making a commitment to doing just that. After a few months of that kind of practice and performance, you will know whether you want to continue that commitment.

But what is "high-level" practicing all about. Bill gives three parts to it.

The first is *fundamentals*. Back in the 60s and 70s Earl Weaver was the manager of the Baltimore Orioles. Weaver was known for preaching one thing over and over- it's the fundamentals that win ball games. You practice the fundamentals until they are routine. Next time you watch a baseball game, notice things like how the first baseman moves to his position to get the ball. It's habit. You watch him throughout the game and you will see him do it the same way almost every time. I have taken hundreds of pictures of pitchers pitching. For each pitcher I very seldom get a picture that is unusual. He always pitches the same way.

Fundamentals.

I didn't ask Bill what he considered fundamentals. I already know the answer:

- Long tones
- Chromatics
- Daily Drills and Technical Studies
- Scales

Google "Bill Adam Trumpet Routine" and you will find the best-known of routines and many variations on it. THAT is fundamentals. Doing them over and over. One is never so good that you don't need to work on some of those early Arban's routines. Herb Alpert told me he plays scales every day. Keeping the fundamentals clear and sharp makes those 10,000 hours effective. If you have an hour to practice, at least 30 minutes of that hour should be fundamentals. I know- we don't have that kind of time. Sure, we do. We find it when we up our level by practicing at high levels.

Bill Bergren's second insight into high-level practicing is to *"slow down."* But Bill, it says allegro! So what. I read on one of the sites I was looking at the other day that if you recognize the tune when playing it, you're not playing it slow enough. Slow down. Make sure you can hit the notes cleanly. Make sure you know what the phrase looks like. Give the phrases feeling- but do it slowly. My one teacher had to keep at me for wanting to play it too fast. I want to be able to show I can do it, that I have the technical chops to succeed at it. But when I do that I always flub up.

Sure we will get faster as time goes on, but it is the ability to play it slowly with meaning and purpose without mistakes that leads to high-level performance.

Finally, repeat, repeat, repeat. *Repetition* is our friend. Don't run it once and forget it. Play it. Then play it again, only better. Build your confidence. Remember the Inner Game tactic of trusting yourself in your playing? Repetition is how you get that confidence.

This isn't deep rocket science or even deep music theory of performance. It is plain old common sense. Which is why we ignore it. We think we have an easier, softer way. We think we can get it done in half the time with half the effort. Well, if it's going to take 10,000 hours no matter how you practice, why not make those 10,000 hours count!

Chapter 1.33

A Day Off?

What you do everyday matters more than what you do every once in a while.

-Gretchen Rubin

Habit: (noun) a settled or regular tendency or practice, especially one that is hard to give up.

After last summer's trumpet camp, I managed to get into an early habit of practice. I had never been that consistent before and it took a while for the habit to sink in. Do it every day, we were told. Make it a habit to play the trumpet every day. One of my notes from our closing session was a quote from someone:

You can take a day off, but you can never get it back.

Then, of course, there's the famous quote attributed to just about every musician who has ever been famous:

> If I miss one day's practice, I notice it. If I miss two days' practice, the critics notice it. If I miss three days' practice, the public notices it.

I was a little concerned, though, since I knew that daily exercise with no breaks is not a good idea in any exercise program from biking to weight-lifting. In fact, it is a cardinal rule of exercise- you need to take a day off in order to allow muscles to rebuild. If I work my upper-body today, I shouldn't work those same muscles tomorrow. Shouldn't this apply to trumpet playing? What about the muscles in my lips and cheeks?

I checked (again) with Bill Bergren and he tried to change my mind on that. He said that the day-off rule is

> not in all forms of exercise. We are building coordination. Trumpet playing has very little to do with strength.

That made a little sense to me, but unlike my work-outs there are just the facial muscles we are working on. I can't work on some and not others. They are muscles, after all.

So I started paying attention to things like how long it takes to get warmed up after a strenuous day of playing. I took note of endurance and range. I began to notice that there were good days and less than good days. Some days I was warmed-up in no time. Other days, I was having trouble getting to "G" above the staff without straining. I made sure that I was taking appropriate breaks while practicing and doing my daily routine- the old "rest as much as you play" rule. Overall, the progress was positive, but not a straight line. Only natural!

This was also after I had been working for nearly 5 months on building my embouchure, endurance, and technique. It wasn't early on so I felt I was in a better place to decipher what was happening.

So when I missed a day of practice, usually due to circumstances, I paid attention to what might have been different. What I discovered was that, in general, one day off like that did not seem to have any major impact. (Denial, maybe?) Sometimes I noticed that the day of rest was actually helpful to my endurance, range, and even tone on the next day. (There probably was something to the idea of a "Sabbath day" after all.) Sometimes my technique would be slightly off, but it usually came back in warm-up.

Then we were traveling and I missed four days in a row. That I noticed. I wasn't back to square one, of course, but I had lost some of the edge. I also was not as on target with my scales or even chromatic runs.

With these experiences I did some more digging on the Internet among some of the many trumpet-based web sites. I found that most do feel that a day off on some regular basis can be helpful. It does allow for some recuperation, especially after a particularly heavy performance or strong of performances. But even those with that view were very clear- taking time off can be dangerous. I pulled out a few "guidelines" from my research:

Take a day off by choice, not laziness- "I don't feel like it today" is not a good reason. As I write this, I have had an easier day. I didn't do my routine- by choice. I had a relatively non-strenuous gig this evening, so for the day I didn't push it since I had a more strenuous day yesterday. It isn't a true day off since I did play this evening, but it was planned this way.

Don't play fatigued- Be aware of the limits of your body. Your muscle memory will work better if it has "good" memories of playing and not memories of how fatigued you were.

Rest as much as you play- this goes with the fatigue issue, but also with the building of endurance.

Do something musical even on the days you don't play- listen to some music, do some study of some music, do some musical research, keep yourself connected to your music.

Don't make it a habit to not play. Yes, you can get by with only 2 or 3 days of practice a week. I have many years experience at that. It doesn't work. You won't improve very quickly and may very likely get frustrated with your lack of progress.

Have fun while practicing. Don't make it a chore- make it a joy. That routine you do every day? It is essential so make it a habit. When it becomes a habit, you will miss it when you don't do it.

So, in general I agree with my friend and mentor, Bill. Daily practice is good and essential. Know that there are times when you can't practice and don't kick yourself if one of those happens. But work at it so it doesn't happen except by accident- or a clear, reasonable choice.

Chapter 1.34

Who Do You Hang With?

I want to be around people that do things. I don't want to be around people anymore that judge or talk about what people do. I want to be around people that dream and support and do things.

— Amy Poehler

Let's be honest- trumpet players have a reputation. (Undeserved, I think. Well, maybe.... Okay, it's complicated.) The old joke:

How does one trumpet player greet another trumpet player?
Hi. I'm better than you.

The implication is very clear. Trumpet players think highly of themselves and believe that any other trumpet player they meet is obviously inferior to them. We might make an exception if we are meeting the first chair of the Chicago Symphony, Doc Severinsen, or the faculty at Shell Lake Trumpet Camp. That's our reputation- and at times- our attitude. I could go into some detail on that, but I will leave that to another time.

The problem with having that attitude is, as you might guess, that we always think we are surrounded by inferior musicians. If we are, each of us, the best around us, that means we have nothing to learn, nowhere to grow, and can become pretty damn obnoxious to be around.

Yes, there are players like that, and they aren't all trumpet players. But overall, my experience has often been that we are often more willing to be in a learning position as in a superior position. Learning takes humility which can be defined as "a willingness to learn." That does not mean that we take an inferior position any more than it means taking a superior position. It means that we enter into each other's musical presence with openness to what we have to learn- as well as share.

One of the quotable lines from Trumpet Camp last summer brought all this to mind:

Surround yourself with people who are better than you are.

I realized that this statement is as much about attitude as it is about musical ability. If you are the first chair in the top group at your school or in your community, chances are that you are a pretty good musician. It may very well be that overall, you might be better than the other people in your section. But the attitude that could come with that can be downright destructive to the group making good music.

And it could get in the way of you discovering new ways of making music yourself.

If any of us project the kind of attitude that says "I'm the best!" the others will wonder what good they are to the group. If that obnoxious first chair looms over the proceedings like the great judge of the universe- I for example will hold back, play more timidly, see my part as a "small" part. Many of us have heard the comeback to that- there are no small parts, only small players. A "superior" musician among us, though, can make us feel "small." The section will never produce good music if that is the case.

In reality, thankfully, these type of trumpet players are few and far between. Oh, admittedly it might not seem that way at first when you hear them play or watch them in action. It is intimidating to many of us to play in a section, especially next to, one of these top-quality players. But once we get to know them, my experience has almost always been one of openness to assist me in growing. It's not about the other trumpet player's attitude- *it's about mine!* With that attitude on our part, we can discover that this otherwise superior musician is weak in a certain area. They minimize the things they are not as proficient at and maximize the things they are good at.

That I can learn from!

When the better player is open to sharing and accepting a role as a leader, which they often are(!), the whole section gets better. I appreciate the section leader who suggests I take a lead that will push me. It says the leader believes I can do it. I will work harder in the group when the section leader gives us all the "Thumbs Up!" after the concert and says we did well because any of us could have played the lead- and played our parts appropriately.

For those who are at least arguably the best player in their section, to take that to heart as grandiosity will get in the way of your ability as well. You will get easily bored and move on if no one else around you has anything to teach you. You can become a prima donna- a very temperamental person with an inflated view of their own talent or importance. You will become a point of dis-sension in your group. You, even as good as you are, could very well contribute to your section or group being less musical.

It is interesting that so often across these months of writing this blog I have moved away from technical musical learning. I have often moved to more gener-al ideas that, applied specifically to trumpet playing can have significant impact. One of these, over and over is summed up in "attitude." And attitudes are choic-es. We can be educated into good or bad attitudes; we can make certain attitudes habits. We all know the perpetual "wet blanket" who never does anything but whine. We also know the cheerleader type who is always up and perky.

These, and all attitudes in-between, will color how we see the world. There's nothing new in saying this. The wisdom is as old as humans who began observing their neighbors' behavior. They then decided they liked being around people with certain behaviors and stayed away from those who others. Or we discover that we may gravitate to those with the same attitude, you know, mis-ery loves company, other people who are as miserable as you are and love to complain about it.

That can be more than just difficult. It can be downright unhealthy and keep us stuck.

Great minds discuss ideas; average minds discuss events; small minds discuss people.

-Eleanor Roosevelt

One more thought came to mind. What if you are the best player around? What if there is no one you can easily get together with that is better than you? I can think of a couple of options.

- Find a teacher in some nearby community who might be willing to take you on as a student. It might not be able to be done weekly, but set up a schedule
- Gather other musicians who would be willing to "jam" or even become a group and push each other. Don't be the "leader". Be just another group member as you seek to blend in with the whole group. Dream with them, have common visions, don't be satisfied for the "good" which is almost always the enemy of both the "better" and the "best" you can be.
- Find camps, workshops, jam sessions, that you can attend.
- Listen, listen, and then listen more to great recordings. All types of recordings. Watch videos online or on the various media. Find lessons online that may be in an area that you are less proficient.
- Go back to the first item and do it again.

It's not always convenient or easy, but if we are committed to being quality musicians, no matter the level of our ability (!!!), we will find the ways.

Chapter 1.35

The World in a Note

The more you get into music, the more you discover that a whole note becomes the whole world.

- Trumpet Camp 2015

The Music Lesson is a wonderful musical philosophy book by bassist Victor Wooten. Early in the book Victor's "mentor" Michael asks him if he remembers the Dr. Seuss book, *Horton Hears a Who*.

"Do you remember what the poor elephant found inside the little speck of dust?"

"There was a whole civilization living inside it."

"Exactly," [Michael] said, pointing at me. "Notes are the same. If you listen closely, you can find a whole world living inside each one. Notes are alive, and like you and me, they need to breathe. The song will dictate how much air is needed."

At the end of trumpet camp last year, we heard the same thing in our closing session as quoted above.

Months ago, as I put together the themes for this blog year, I sent Mr. Baca an email asking for an explanation, a line or two that I could riff on. He was always too busy.

Actually, I think he was doing me a favor. He was letting me figure it out on my own. I would schedule a post on the subject, then push it back. A few weeks ahead, I would say,

"Nope, Mr. Baca hasn't answered me yet."

I would push it back again. It seems I needed to discover the world in a note for myself.

To understand how the world exists in a single note is not something that can be clearly taught. It is one of those things that makes sense only when you have your "Aha!" moment. I've been given clues and ideas about what it means, but, hey, I can be a little slow. The answer was right in front of me all the time. It was shown over and over on web sites and articles. It showed up every day I picked up my horn to practice.

A couple weeks ago it came to me. Clear as the bell on my trumpet. It came together when watching a video of Wynton Marsalis on the website- Arban Method. (arbanmethod.com/wynton-marsalis-long-tones/)

Long tones. The boring, bane of every trumpet player.

I remembered Mr. Baca at Big Band Camp telling me to take the tuning slide off and just play that single tone.

- Play it;
- listen to the sound;
- center it;
- hold it;
- just let the air go through;
- listen to the sound;
- keep it centered;
- Now do it again.

In that note is the whole world of trumpet music. In that note will be every note you play.

Now, put the slide back in and do it with "G". It's still there. THAT note hasn't changed. The trumpet does the work.

Play up the scale. Every note is still that single buzzing tone- the single note of the world. Play down the scale. The same thing is happening.

With every long tone, you play that same single tone. It is, in essence, the foundation of every note on the horn. As long as you keep that in mind, and the physics and philosophy of the buzz note, you will have the whole scale.

How simple.

One of our local PBS stations is currently rerunning the Ken Burns series *Jazz*. It's amazing how much different the series is 16 years after first aired. I am hearing and seeing things that were irrelevant to me when I first saw it. In last week's episode one of the commentators was discussing the revolutionary genius of Louis Armstrong. (An understatement!) He was describing how Armstrong took "pop" songs and interpreted them for his jazz bands. No one else was doing that. They played them straight. Armstrong, the commentator said, went to the very essence of the songs. He would often distill it all to one note (!) playing the tempo and swinging the groove. One note! The whole song in that single note.

When I started this trumpet journey last summer, I thought the purpose of doing long tones was to build chops. If I did long tones on a regular basis I would improve the embouchure, increase my range, build endurance, develop breath, and learn to center each note. All of which is true. But now I have a hunch these are the important results of finding the whole world in the single note on the horn.

Most instrumentalists face the same task. We can't make chords on our instruments like a pianist or guitarist (or even banjo player) can. We have one note at a time to work with. At first we learn the notes. We discover the ways to play each individual note. It has its place on the scale and we play it. We do our version of "chords" when we move to intervals, playing thirds and arpeggios. But it is still only one note at a time. (Ignore overtones for this discussion.)

Somewhere along the line we begin to hear differently. We begin to discover the world in our trumpet, the voice we talked about in an earlier post that is uniquely ours.

And it's all in that single note we can only play one at a time.

Let's move away from music for a moment and get philosophical. My goal in this blog is as much to "tune" our individual lives as it is to "tune" our musical chops. This is as true for who we are and what we hope to do or be each and every day. That single, buzzing "G" is our individual core. It is our personality, our skills, our hopes and dreams. If we try to focus too much on these and seek all the answers, we will quickly become unfocused. Our lives simply responding to the next "thing" or next "crisis" or even next "dream."

But what is your "G" tone? What is your world in a single note at the center of your soul? What's in your heart? How does that define what you can do and how you do it? Take the time to center on that. Meditate on it. Learn to live it and let it guide you no matter what is happening.

Chapter 1.36

Musician Heroes

Without heroes, we're all plain people and don't know how far we can go.

-Bernard Malamud

I am going to take a side journey away from the trumpet alone this week. A number of times over these weeks I have talked about who we listen to and who we surround ourselves with as important parts of our lives as musicians. As a result, we often develop strong emotional connections with famous musicians we have never met.

I have spent a great deal of time in the past two weeks reflecting on the role of music and top musicians in my world. It was kicked off by the sudden death of the pop superstar, Prince. But it is something that has been raised countless times over the years whenever one of our great musicians dies. We have had our share already this year of the loss of these greats, Prince being the latest and, sadly, not the last.

We often call these people like Prince "icons." A definition of icon can be:

A person or thing regarded as a representative symbol of something or

Someone who is venerated or idolized.

For better or worse, many of these musicians we uphold as heroes and icons *are* people we "idolize." Many of the "greats" do also inspire us and can lead us to greater things. As musicians we have the heroes of our own instruments that we love to emulate. I still get joy as I continue to work on Al Hirt's "Java" or play Herb Alpert's "Spanish Flea" in the big band. These spur me to play my best along with transcribing or just plain listening to some of the great solos of trumpet history.

Another piece of the musicians we hold as "icons" can be our part in the greater culture around us. These are the musicians who were the soundtrack for our lives at particular times and places. The most deeply ingrained are those whose music connects with strong and emotional memories. We "grew up" to that music. It is "our music." No one can ever take that away- it is imprinted in our memory. The way memory works, it is also directly linked to people, places, feelings. The opening vamp on the Four Tops "Reach Out I'll Be There" instantly transports me back to the radio station my freshman year at college. I can see it, smell it, react to is as if I were sitting there.

Which is why the death of a Prince, Merle Haggard, or David Bowie hits so close to home. The many ways people remember Prince are as much about ourselves as they are about Prince's musicianship, though naturally he wouldn't have had the cultural impact if he wasn't so talented.

This struck me when I stopped by Paisley Park in Chanhassen, MN, last week. One of the items left as a memorial was a baseball hat from an Iraq War veteran. Perhaps Prince's music carried him through his time in Iraq. Maybe it was the only way he remained connected with home and hope at difficult times. I don't know, but just seeing it there was a powerful spiritual moment, connecting this time and place with others. I was humbled by that.

Which brings me around to you and me- musicians ourselves. Someone reading this today may one day be of the stature of an important musician impacting the greater culture. Most of us will not. We will play our music to keep our lives connected to this force we call music. It will be how we maintain our balance and discover new ways to express ourselves.

But- and this is important- we may never be "icons" but we *will* continue to have an impact on those for whom we play. Music, overall, is a spiritual language that connects us to our audiences. It is a conduit for getting in touch with something far greater than ourselves that is at the heart of human experience. No, I don't believe I am overstating this. We have all had it happen to us when listening to music- and when playing or performing music.

One of the big bands I play with, regularly plays at senior living facilities in the area. The joy on people's faces is priceless. Seeing a person who barely moves, tap a foot ever so subtly to the beat is why it is important. Our band, at that moment, is as important to that person's life as Prince was to many other lives. We have heard from staff members at some of these facilities about changes in residents after we have played there. They are lifted, encouraged, happier.

That is why we do what we do as musicians. We are, in countless and unknown ways, opening the window for the possibility of the spiritual entering our presence.

When speaking of religious icons, a definition I remember from a TV series many years ago was something or someone that opens a vision of God or the spiritual.

We can be that icon for others through our music. Music, of course, is not the only way this happens, but it is one of the ways we as musicians can participate in the expansion of the spiritual in the world. It is at that point that we move beyond ourselves into the flowing of that which is greater than us and sharing it around us.

I am honored and humbled to be able to do that.

Chapter 1.37

The Reality of Dreams

If one advances confidently in the direction of his dreams, and endeavors to live the life which he has imagined, he will meet with a success unexpected in common hours.

-Henry David Thoreau

A month or so ago I came across a group of people going door-to-door for some cause or other. I was polite and said, "Hello. How are things going?" The answer was a kind of sarcastic, almost fatalistic, "Living the dream!"

Huh? I just went on my way- as did they.

A couple days ago I was talking to a fellow trumpet player who asked about my involvement in groups and my regular routine. After telling him he responded, "Well, that *is* being a musician full-time."

I smiled and said that this has been a dream of mine for years- to be a "full-time musician. Finally, with semi-retirement, I'm doing it."

When I stop and think about that statement I am still taken aback. What right does a 67-year-old retired pastor and semi-retired counselor have to think he can be a "full-time musician?" Even though I don't need to do it to make a living, is it realistic? Isn't it naïve to think it is possible or should even be worth doing?

One of the quotes I wrote down at the end of trumpet camp last summer was:

The reality of dreams comes from naive ideas.

Simply put, even to think some of our dreams are possible is an act of naive belief. As usual, I like to look at definitions and found these two for naive:

- showing a lack of experience, wisdom, or judgment.
- natural and unaffected; innocent.

Most times when we dream of things we would like to do or become there is a definite lack of experience. It is naive in that we don't know what it means or even how to get there. It sounds impossible. We may be told, "Get real!"

A lack of experience, wisdom and judgment, however, can easily lead to the second definition- innocent. Many dreams have a simple, joyful aspect to them. They are based on innocent belief that this might just very well be possible. It can be found in that age-old question, "What do you want to be when you grow up?" I once wanted to be an astronaut. But it wasn't a dream. Just a sense of adventure. I also dreamed of being a youth worker, a counselor, a preacher, a radio announcer and a TV host/producer. Those were dreams.

As a result, I have been ALL of these at times in the past 50 years. I found ways to make all those naive dreams into reality.

I have also dreamed of being a musician. I never let go of that one. Things often got in the way- like earning a living, time commitments, etc. But I never let the trumpet go. Whenever and however I could, I found ways to keep playing, however sporadic or mediocre it was at times.

The subject is dreams and believing in them as possible. This is all about the reality of dreams beginning in naive innocence and growing into existence.

When researching this post I came across a blog by Joey Tartell, an Associate Professor of Trumpet and the Director of Undergraduate Studies at Indiana

University's Jacobs School of Music. In a post titled "Belief" (https://joeytartell.com/2012/05/01/belief/) he had this to say:

> Last week, in a lesson, I told a student that I knew she could play the piece in question great. But the look I got back from her reminded me of the second hardest part of teaching:
>
> There are times where the teacher has more belief in the student than the student has in her/himself....
>
> Which brings me back to belief. It's a very difficult concept to teach. Try this: picture a player that you admire. Now you need to know that that player was once a beginner. That player was not born playing at a world class level. That player had to learn fundamentals and music just like everyone else. And on the first day of playing did not sound like a professional. So if that player can do it, why not you?

Belief in oneself is at the heart of turning dreams into reality. Belief is based on your dreams and the reality those dreams represent. Belief is based on what you think you are able to accomplish, what your skills are and, just as importantly, what your skills can develop into!

Back when I was talking about the Inner Game of Music, I wrote the following:

> Self-trust. Do you believe you can do it? Have you worked on being able to do it? Have you set goals, formal or informal to be ready to do it? Have you allowed you and the music to meld into a unique idea? If so, you can do it.
>
> If not, don't quit, just go back and work some more. But remember, sooner or later we will have to be ready. Do it. You know you can.

That is belief and it is basic to overcoming the inner barriers we place in our own way. Such trust and belief is what we build as we practice, develop helpful and healthy routines, begin to develop our skills into new levels of experience and even expertise. This is where those routines and experiences, the people we hang around with, the story we discover in ourselves and the song we sing come together. In our dreams and the belief we can live them.

Joey Tartell concludes his post:

So here's what I need for you to do:

- Dream big. Think of what you want to do, not what you'd settle for.
- Realize that someone gets to do that, so it could be you.
- Get working, because it's unlikely anyone is just going to hand it to you. You need to earn it.
- But most importantly, believe in the possibility. Like most things, this becomes a logic problem for me. So, follow me here:
- If you don't believe, your chances of success are virtually zero.
- If you believe, your chances are now higher than zero just based on the acceptance of the possibility of success.

(https://joeytartell.com/2012/05/01/belief/)

Chapter 1.38

Logic or Emotions

Music is the shorthand of emotion.

— Leo Tolstoy

Yeah, but what did Tolstoy know? The music that is arguably the most amazing in western history is the music of Johann Sebastian Bach- and it is some of the most logical music ever written. Mathematically precise; ordered in almost uncanny exactness. No wonder that when Wendy Carlos (under her birth name of Walter Carlos) wanted to show the amazing use of the Moog Synthesizer, she used the music of Bach. (*Switched on Bach.* 1968.) There should be no emotion in a computer-generated song; no human input to play it other than the 1s and 0s of computer/digital coding.

Yet it was an amazing album that touched people deeply, and not just because of the newness and uniqueness of it. For many of us who first heard it in 1968, the album, for example, captured the emotion of *Jesu, Joy of Man's Desiring* with amazing clarity.

Logic will get you from A to B. Imagination will take you everywhere.

- Albert Einstein

As much as mathematical precision, Bach also used imagination that allowed him to place layer upon layer of things never before seen or heard. The imagination of Wendy Carlos added another layer which grabbed us like nothing ever seen or heard before. Yet it was all there in Bach's logic combined with his musical imagination.

Then we have Miles Davis on *Kind of Blue* or John Coltrane on *A Love Supreme*. At one moment their solos can sound as precise as Bach's mathematical journeys. The next moment, then, is filled with an emotion that sweeps in and takes over, surrounding us with things that are like nothing ever seen or heard before. All of us who work with music from the rank amateur to the amazing heights of Davis or Coltrane know that everything they do is based on all the logical manipulations of music theory. They may twist those theories and make up a few new ones of their own, but they are acutely aware of the logic behind what they are doing.

A mind all logic is like a knife all blade. It makes the hand bleed that uses it.
- Rabindranath Tagore

It is no doubt obvious where I am going with this. We are not dealing with an either/or situation when we deal with logic and emotion. It must be a both/ and for it to go beyond just the notes on the page or in our heads. In human thinking it used to be that we believed that if only we humans would be "logical," then we would always make the right decisions. When faced with choices, we should be able to use the coolness and precision of logic to make the good choices.

Without going into all the details, science, medicine, and psychology were all shocked when this proved to be an incorrect theory. There were examples where a person, through an injury or surgery, lost the ability to connect emotions to decision making. All their decisions were based on good old-fashioned rational thinking. "Just the facts!" The old theory would say that their decisions post-trauma should have been better decisions- emotions weren't in the picture.

144

That is not what happened. In essence, they actually lost some of the critical ability to make any decisions in the first place. Neuroscience had to be rewritten. Cold, impersonal logic does not make good decisions alone. To disconnect emotion is to take away what makes us human- and what makes human decision-making human in the first place.

Which is why I think music has played such an essential and foundational role in human culture and development. Daniel Levitan, neuroscientist, session musician, sound engineer, and record producer, captured this idea in his two seminal works, *This Is Your Brain on Music: The Science of a Human Obsession and The World in Six Songs: How the Musical Brain Created Human Nature*. Somewhere in our brain, music, I think, brings together emotion and logic in ways very few things do.

Music expresses that which cannot be put into words and that which cannot remain silent.

— Victor Hugo

So, let's get back to you and me and how this is important to us. Actually, in some ways it is another way of reminding us of things already discussed and beginning to put them into a "logical", effective, and helpful place.For example, we have talked about being able to be aware of, and able to share, "your story" in your music. How do you know your story? By your feelings, among other things, and then applying logic and thinking to it. We discussed the importance of the "groove" in music. Well, first we have to have the "logical" ability to play the notes correctly. Then we add the feeling, the emotion we are sensing in the notes. That becomes the groove.

That's why we practice. First to find the notes- the specifics of this song in this place. Then we find the groove- the story, the emotions, the nuances. These are built on the logic of knowing the fundamentals as well as how we are feeling. We may be able to play a piece with clockwork precision, but does it "feel?" It is in the feeling that we connect with the music.

Am I just repeating the same thing over and over, driving it into the ground until you say, "Enough already! We get it."? Perhaps, but I have found over the past year that I forget these things on a regular basis. I get bogged down in the notes on the page or the dynamic markings. I forget to listen to the music as I am playing it in my practice room. I rush through the notes instead of listening to them; I try to get the piece down cold in one or two attempts; I don't savor the world found in each note. Or, in performance, I can ignore the other musicians I am playing with. Sometimes I get so emotionally involved in a song that, without me realizing it I get sloppy and the technique can get lost.

I have to be constantly reminded of the interaction of logic and emotion- unless the emotion I want to drag out of the horn, myself, or the listener is disgust. It is in the balance of our logic and emotion that practice turns into performance, that we discover how a particular song can express our own story.

Don't let your logic close out your emotions- or your feelings dismiss logic. Together they make quite a duet.

Chapter 1.39

Letting Go- A Reminder

The key to change... is to let go of fear.

-Rosanne Cash

Letting go means taking risks.

Letting go is taking action, not resisting

Controlling comes from fear - if I am not in charge, things will fall apart.

From Bill Ferguson's *Mastery of Life*:

> Fear is a state of mind and is created by resisting a future event. For example, if you have a fear of losing someone, you are resisting the future event called, "losing the person." The more you resist losing the person, the bigger your fear. The bigger your fear, the more you feel threatened. The more you feel threatened, the more you hang on and push the person away. By resisting the future event, you tend to make the fear come true. (*How to let go and flow with life.*) ([http://www.](http://www.masteryoflife.com/letgo.html) [masteryoflife.com/letgo.html](http://www.masteryoflife.com/letgo.html))

In a business organization book, *Yes to the Mess*, Frank J. Barrett relates being part of a jazz combo to successful business practices. Letting go is part of it:

> Jazz musicians... often speak of letting go of deliberation and control. They employ deliberate, conscious attention in their practice, but at the moment when they are called upon to play, this conscious striving becomes an obstacle. Too much regulation and control restrict the emergence of fresh ideas. To get jazz right, musicians must surrender their conscious striving...

We're back to the practice room again. A natural place to start the process of letting go. We strive in practice and let go in performance. He is of course talking about improvising, but for most of us this letting go begins with any public performance.

> In the words of saxophonist Ken Peplowski, "You carry along all the scales and all the chords you learned, and then you take an intuitive leap into the music. Once you take that leap, you forget all about those tools. You just sit back and let divine intervention take over."

I'm not sure about "divine intervention" in my trumpet playing. I'm not sure that God cares that much about what I play. My interpretation is that when I get in touch with the "spiritual" aspect of playing music, I can more easily let go and allow the music to flow.

But there is another aspect of all this letting go. Unless we are in a solo recital, we do not play alone in public performance. Whether it is a duo or trio, a combo or a wind band, our music has to fit into what the others are playing. Hence the statement I saw on Facebook one day:

> Practice is to learn your part;
> Rehearsal is to learn the other parts
> and how your part fits in.

Wisdom.

But the letting go is really in the next step, the actual public performance. The time when nerves and stage fright, performance anxiety and just plain old "blanking out" takes over.

Here I have to make a confession: I have a very difficult time practicing what I preach when I get into a solo performance. I know I have talked about this before, but it has raised its ugly countenance again. I had some pieces down cold- in my practice room. I got to rehearsal psyched to play- and it was like I had never seen the piece before.

Damn!

Now, to be good to myself, I have made progress. I can play in the quintet and not get that fear. I can play in the concert band and, for the most part, allow my part to sing out. But the solos are still bugging me.

I do know that the techniques of letting go work. They have worked for me. I know from experience that letting go can move me to new places. I also know that what Frank Barrett talks about above are the problems:

Striving-

which means working hard instead of relaxing

Regulation and control-

wanting to remain in charge and not trust the flow of the music

Tense muscles-

caused by the inner tension and growing uncertainty

Shallow breathing-

when we are tense, we don't take the time to deeply breathe. We react and the fear cycle of fight or flight kicks in.

Losing attention-

and then we are in full time crisis mode.

I have talked about all these things in the past. But they bear repeating and relearning. The need to "Let Go" at those moments is essential. Taking a deep breath, realigning yourself (easier to do if you're not in the middle of a solo!), focus on what is in front of you.

This is simple. I wish it were as easy!

With time, it may be.

Chapter 1.40

Losing My Mojo- A Cautionary Tale

Many of our deepest motives come, not from an adult logic of how things work in the world, but out of something that is frozen from childhood.

-Kazuo Ishiguro

There was a time somewhere over half a century ago when I was your typical high school trumpet player. I no doubt believed I was invincible, the top of the band's musical food chain. My sight-reading ability was somewhat lacking, but one evening of working on it at home usually fixed that and I was able to exhibit the skill that my first chair position would expect.

I don't remember any hints of uncertainty or doubts about what I could do as a trumpet player. I was lead trumpet in our stage musical. I organized a small combo to play at our school talent show and even made an arrangement of the Beatles' *Help!* As our number. I was lead in a trumpet quartet that played at many local churches. I was also lead in a Tijuana Brass-style group that played at both the local pool and at our town's annual Fourth of July fest. I knew I would never be a professional musician- that wasn't in my plans. I did know that I loved being a trumpet player.

I had what I might later have called "mojo."

For over fifty years, I have considered Memorial Day as the day I lost it. True or not, what we believe is often "truth" if not "fact." If we believe *it, it* is real. Since today is the 50th Anniversary of that day, I will tell the story in full, something I have wanted to do for years.

The "Monday Holiday" bill had not yet been enacted. In 1966 Memorial Day, the day to remember those who died in battle, always celebrated on May 30, happened to fall on a Monday. It was a mostly clear, cool morning. I remember a misty fog along the river, not unusual on a spring morning like that. The sun was breaking through as I joined the group of veterans at the corner of Main and Allegheny Streets on the bank of the West Branch of the Susquehanna River.

Memorial Day always began at the river. This was a time to remember the sailors who had died in service. Since we were only a couple decades past the end of World War II the memories were personal, real and not yet part of history. They were still at the edge of current events.

It was a simple ceremony. I don't know what was said. I remember what was done. A reading and a prayer, and a wreath tossed solemnly into the river. The honor guard rifles faced up-river, to the right in the above picture, and proceeded with the traditional three-volley salute. The volley comes from the battlefield tradition of three-volleys to indicate that the dead had been removed from the battlefield and properly cared for.

The sounds echoed from the mountains and it was my turn.

Taps.

My notes felt right. They flowed as I wanted them to. They moved up-river following the smoke from the volleys. It was an honor to be called to do this. My friend Steve, the second chair, was stationed a short distance away to play the echo. It was all moving and appropriate. It was finished.

Next Steve and I joined the rest of our high school marching band for the parade. Having just graduated, it would be our last official home town parade. The parade moved up the main east-west street through town.

We marched past what had been my Dad's pharmacy and then our house. We went by the junior high school where a Winged Victory statue remembered World War 1 sacrifices. Just past my grandfather's house a small curve in the street took us up hill to the left-turn that led into the cemetery. The band took its "parade rest"-style position for the ceremony.

Speeches and honors were now given for all who had died in the service of the country. For a small-town in Central Pennsylvania, we had our share of names on the veterans' memorials downtown next to the Post Office. There were 45 who died from World War II, and another 9 from Korea. Many hundreds served.

But that's another story.

My memory of that day is fixed with what happened next. The three-volley honor salute was finished. It was not the first time I had been in this cemetery and heard that. This was my fourth or fifth Memorial Day parade. Beyond that, my dad, a veteran of WW II, had died about 18 months earlier. The volley had echoed from the hilltop cemetery on that cold December day. Now I was standing but twenty yards or so from his and my mother's graves,

Again, time to play *Taps*. I was focused and ready to go. *Taps* is not difficult to play. It is ingrained in every trumpet player's mind. Its haunting sound is as familiar as our own name. Steve had gone to the hilltop behind us for his echo response to my call.

Perhaps I was nervous, or, at the other extreme, over-confident. I don't remember any performance anxiety at that time. This was not my first public solo performance. Most likely I was just careless.

Three notes in I choked. Everything I knew about performing disappeared. I had forgotten to let the water out of the horn. The sound started to gurgle, the notes lost their clear intensity. My mind went into auto-pilot, which 50 years ago did not include the simple act of letting the water out in one of the pauses at the end of a phrase.

I finished with the gurgles seeming to mock me even more intensely when Steve's echo sounded so perfect to my ear. I was upset at myself. I had let the veterans down. I had let my father down.

I was ashamed.

I had one more opportunity. There was one more short parade that afternoon in nearby Salladasburg. There was one more cemetery with *Taps*.

That, too, became an embarrassment. I flubbed a note at the beginning and, yes, I again forgot to let the water out. That, I am sure, was more nerves and, even more likely, inexperience.

But it became *my* experience. It became, for me, a defining moment in my musical life. It made me, in my mind, a sloppy trumpet player. One day in May 1966 set a standard of self-understanding that I have spent half a century trying to change. My low sight-reading skills added to it three months later when I did not pass the audition to get into the marching band at college. I never thought until recently that they simply didn't need another freshman trumpet player at that point and it had nothing to do with my ability. The Memorial Day experience was already coloring my personal lowering expectations.

A couple posts ago I wrote how logic and emotions interact. My now ancient story is as good an example as I can imagine. In the great scheme of things, even the past 50 years of my own life, that Memorial Day series of flubs isn't even a drop in the bucket. If anyone noticed then, or remembers it today, I would be shocked. I did what I could and I did it well. My logical brain knows all that. It knows that the gurgling sound of a trumpet is not the end of the world- and that very few people even heard it.

But there was a sense of failure and shame connected to that moment in my memory. It had more to do with standing mere yards from my parents' graves than it did about the hundred or so people who were there. It was connected with my own needs to live up to perfection for my deceased parents. In that moment I failed.

Here's how that all works in us. We start with:

- **Principles:**

-Values
-What you stand for
-Your personal foundation

These don't change much over our lives. They are reaffirmed or adjusted, but we mostly maintain our personal principles.

We add to our lives with:

- **Experiences:**

  - What happens to you
  - Interactions with the world beyond you

In and of themselves, these experiences are simply there. We give them meaning, positive or negative, healthy or unhealthy, based on our personal values, that foundation through which we judge the world and ourselves. This then produces:

- **Emotions:**

  - Feelings at a given moment.
  - Reactions to experiences

Let's put it together:

- Experiences produce emotions.
- These emotions may be based on our principles and values, or on a physical reaction to what is happening. If it makes us feel good, happy, fulfilled or whatever, it is a positive emotion. If we are hurt, sad, lost, etc. it can be a negative emotion.
- Experiences and emotions are stored together in our memory.
- That's how memories work. They are not stored as a single event- A Memory in A Location. They are stored in some interconnected way in our brain. When a memory comes back it easily comes back with the emotions. This is Proust's famous experience with the madeleine cake.

- The emotions connected with experiences can then interact with our principles.
- Good emotions can produce a positive "value" response; negative feeling emotions can produce a "value" response that says that this does not fit my values.
- Together, these guide how we do what we do in our lives.

To design the future effectively, you must first let go of your past.

-Charles J. Givens

There's the rub. Back again to the letting go I talked about last week. Back to logic and emotion and principles and mindfulness.

After a previous post on developing experiences my friend Terry commented:

Experience counts more than theory, because experience works on the heart

But when that work on the heart is an ongoing emotional "shame" it will color what we do every time we are faced with a similar situation.

Finally, today, 50 years later, I am discovering new ways to rewrite that emotional experience of Memorial Day 1966. I have been able over the past few years specifically, to present alternative realities. I have also been willing to take risks such as doing a solo, attending jazz, big band, and trumpet camps where I couldn't hide and playing in a quintet. New experiences rewrite the "heart story" and put things into a better perspective. Even this Tuning Slide blog on trumpet playing is part of it.

I have been controlled by that previous day for 50 years. Maybe I will finally let it go.

Chapter 1.41

Finding New Comfort

Anxiety, it just stops your life.

-Amanda Seyfried

No, I'm not going to talk about anxiety as such. I'm going to talk about how we have learned to deal with it. We all know what it is, of course. But here's one definition:

Anxiety:

a feeling of

- worry,

- nervousness, or

-unease,

typically, about an imminent event or something with an uncertain outcome.

One of our natural adaptations to the world around us is our response to anxiety producing times and places. When we face a situation of perceived fear or threat there are survival mechanisms that come into play.

Maureen Werrbach, MA, LCPC writes about this on Psych Central:

> ...your body is responding to a perceived threat. This is called the stress response. The stress responses, fight, flight, or freeze, help us in situations where we perceive physical or mental threat. (Original post was from 2014. I accessed it in 2016. It is no longer available that I could find.)

Right there they are:

- Fight
- Flight
- Freeze.

They are the things of anxiety that can "stop your life." They are essential responses to life-threatening situations. The problem is that they developed when almost everything in the world around us was a life-threatening situation. That rustling of the leaves in the bush was more likely a predator than a small bird. High-level awareness was a necessity to remaining alive. What is even more important is that these responses occurred deep in the early human brain, beneath consciousness. These responses were, and are, hard-wired into who we are. These initial responses would occur in a fraction of a second before the conscious mind knew what was happening.

We still have that going on. If you are standing on the sidewalk and suddenly a car veers out of control heading at you, your mid-brain response may be as long as .2 to .3 seconds before your conscious brain knows it is happening. You will probably jump out of the way. This will happen before you know with your conscious mind that it is happening.

Two-tenths of a second doesn't seem like very long. But a vehicle moving at even 40 mph will travel about 60 feet (!) in one second. In that .2 - .3 seconds it will travel 12 - 18 feet. That may be just enough time for you to jump to safety.

You probably knew that you couldn't fight the vehicle. But you may have some background that causes you to freeze instead of flee, which is fatal.

The kind of threats that our ancestors faced, though, are much less common than they used to be. We don't have wild animals stalking us, for example. Our lives, in much of the world, in spite of what we often feel or hear, are far safer on a day-to-day basis than they have ever been. As a result, we have developed ways of evaluating anxiety-producing situations and easing the fears and sub-conscious responses. Throughout our lives we develop these self-soothing mechanisms. They are defense mechanisms against things we don't like to feel, don't have to feel, or don't want to feel. When we enter into an anxious place where fear, worry, nervousness or unease bubble up, we all have ways we have learned to cope with these. Therefore, these situations bring old issues up- old ways of finding safety or comfort. Even if they have become counter-productive!!

They are automatic thoughts!

We have all kinds of automatic thoughts going on all the time. They are like the trailer at the bottom of the TV screen during a ball game. While the game is happening on the screen, the trailer is telling you about other games, scores, etc. Our automatic thoughts are that trailer. Which means we don't pay much attention to them unless we have to.

If, in the middle of that ball game, you hear a "ping" or "beep" that is out of place you will most likely see something like a severe weather warning down in the trailer section. The "automatic thoughts" of the trailer are now conscious. You read the warning- and you miss the game-winning touchdown as the clock runs out. In spite of what we think we can do; multi-tasking is next to impossible.

When these thoughts are "negative" and get in the way we refer to them as "Automatic Negative Thoughts"- or ANTs. That can be a way of identifying them and putting them into a healthier place in our mind.

Every time you are tempted to react in the same old way, ask if you want to be a prisoner of the past or a pioneer of the future.

~Deepak Chopra

But these automatic thoughts, negative or positive, are how our brains work. They are finely tuned for survival- and anxiety is a sign that something feels threatening- or at least uncomfortable and we want to change it. Which brings us back to

- fight
- flight or
- freeze.

I have spent years working in addiction counseling and treatment. For some people the anxiety response they have developed over the years is to drink or use chemicals. They are seeking comfort from, ease of the anxiety and fears. It becomes the default response. They are not even aware how it happened or, at times, even why. It has become hard-wired. It is a "flight" response. Escape. Get away.

That is an extreme example, but the way it happens is similar to the many other ways we respond. Here are some other ways:

- **Flight:** not taking solos because of anxiety; dropping out of the group since you can't "keep up"
- **Fight:** always be a rebel and a trouble-maker; be unwilling to accept what someone else is suggesting because it makes you uncomfortable; passive-aggressive responses can be just as much "fight" as some overt action.
- **Freeze:** Not responding to a suggestion, keep doing what you have always done and ignore the ideas. (This can look like passive-aggressive, but is different in attitude.)

When these become habitual, they are also chemically wired in the per-conscious mid-brain. Does this mean we are now stuck in these old ways of dealing with these situations and feelings? Fortunately, the answer is no. One of the discoveries of neuroscience is that the brain is quite "plastic," It can "rewire" itself. If it couldn't a person who had a stroke could never learn to walk or talk again. The brain develops work arounds. We can help that process.

Actually, we have to or it won't happen. That is the purpose of physical therapy/rehab after a stroke or traumatic brain injury. That is the purpose of recovery activities for an addict. These help the brain rewire itself in more healthy ways. Learning anxiety work arounds will help our brains move beyond the ways we have always done it and find new sources of comfort in anxious times.

On the Psych Central website mentioned earlier, Maureen Werrbach suggested these proven methods.

- **Embrace imperfection.** Striving for perfection always leads to stress. Practice replacing perfectionistic thinking with more acceptable, less extreme ones.

- **Identify automatic thoughts.** Uncover the meaning of these thoughts and you can begin to replace them with more appropriate thoughts.

- **Become a neutral observer.** Stop looking at the stressful situation through your emotion-filled lens. Imagine that your stressful thoughts are someone else's. You will notice that you can see things more objectively this way.

- **Practice breathing exercises.** Focus your attention on your breath. Fill your lungs slowly and exhale slowly for a count of 10. Start over if you lose count. This exercise is meant to reduce your body's response to stress.

- **Accept and tolerate life events.** Acknowledge, endure, and accept what is happening in your life at the moment. Focus on the present and be mindful of your surroundings. Be deliberate about allowing this exact moment to be what it is, rather than what you wish or hope it to be.

Don't expect an immediate, extreme change. Anxiety and stress response habits are as ingrained as any other long-term habit. But as we learn the newer responses and practice them as needed, they will slowly but surely become our new comfort and new normal.

One final quote I found:

P.S. You're not going to die. Here's the white-hot truth: if you go bankrupt, you'll still be okay. If you lose the gig, the lover, the house, you'll still be okay. If you sing off-key, get beat by the competition, have your heart shattered, get fired...it's not going to kill you. Ask anyone who's been through it.

~Danielle LaPorte

Chapter 1.42

Crazy Great!

Learning isn't a way of reaching one's potential but rather a way of developing it."

— Anders Ericsson

A recently published book has been making some waves. In *Peak: Secrets from the New Science of Expertise* by Anders Ericsson (psychologist) and Robert Pool (science writer)...

> skillfully examine the eternal debate of nature vs. nurture with this thoughtful treatise supporting the latter. The authors posit that deliberate, focused practice is the key to learning and mastering any new skill, whether or not an underlying natural talent is present. "Generally, the solution is not 'try harder,' but 'try differently,'"

-Publishers Weekly (http://www.publishersweekly.com/978-0-544-45623-5)

Success in today's world, expertise, requires a focus on practical performance, not just the accumulation of information.

I thought this would be an appropriate way to end this first year of the Tuning Slide. It gets back to the general themes we have looked at in these posts since last September. It deals with intention, practice, passion, having mentors, paying attention. Anders and Pool comment that they

> *..can report with confidence that I have never found a convincing case for anyone developing extraordinary abilities without intense, extended practice.*

The students of Bill Adam's instruction (and their students!) who have so influenced me this past year would agree. They have challenged me, and through me, you to look more closely at what we do in practice. Take it seriously. Find the time if you want to find the skills. Over this past year, as I have shared with you my journey at age 67 to become a much more proficient trumpet player this has been my constant awareness. Each month I found myself practicing more days- because I wanted to and made it happen. Each month I also practiced longer each day- again because I wanted to and had the increased ability to do so. There are now days when I finish my routine and practice and can't believe what I have managed. Old dogs- new tricks. Yep!

As Anders and Pool tell us:

> *Doing the same thing over and over again in exactly the same way is not a recipe for improvement; it is a recipe for stagnation and gradual decline.*

If I keep doing what I have always done I will keep getting what I have always gotten. Sure, I may have more endurance, but I won't have gained much else. One thing I know I want to work on, for example, is my high-note ability. I have a hunch I have been working on that the way I have always worked on it. Yes, I am more able to hit the high "C" than I used to be, but it is not solid or clear. My experience tells me I am not finding new ways to work on it to get me past my plateau. One of my goals this summer at adult Big Band Camp is to find one of the instructors who can help me figure that out.

Meanwhile, don't stop practicing and growing. It is easy in the summer to become distracted. If you want to continue to grow toward your expertise, keep at it. (I will have more to say about Anders and Pool's important book in year two.)

Let me conclude with two paragraphs from the website, *Create Yourself Today* about the Anders and Pool book. This is Angela's takeaway from it

> It's not what you are born with or not, that makes you great at anything, makes your performance peak. And it's not your environment either, at least not the one you were born into.
>
> Your performance at any given field is all about your intent, your readiness, your desire to get great. Exceptionally great.
>
> (http://www.createyourself.today/talent-is-way-overrated-peak-secrets-from-the-new-science-of-expertise-by-anders-ericsson-and-robert-pool/)

Maybe even

Crazy good to great!

Year Two

How You Do Anything- Moving On

As I was getting ready to start Year Two a friend gave me a quote which had significantly impacted his life. I used it in the second post of the new year. It became my theme of this second year of the Tuning Slide blog posts. It is simple, but when taken seriously it can be a transformational idea.

The way you do anything is how you do everything!

Think about it and keep it in mind as you follow along in this second stage of my journey as a musician applying the lessons to everyday life.

Chapter 2.1

Being a Trumpet Player

Today I start volume two of The Tuning Slide. I come refreshed with new ideas from another Shell Lake Trumpet Workshop week. I have been doing some exciting reading and experiencing insights into music, life, and the connections they make.

Over this past year I have found myself moving from an okay amateur trumpet player into a somewhat more accomplished amateur. I have spent more time practicing and playing than I ever would have thought possible. As the year progressed, I found it more and more difficult to MISS a day of practice. Since mid-April, I have only missed one day- a long day of travel and meetings. As a result, I have discovered that you can teach an old dog new tricks.

In some of my reading I came across a fun and insightful description of trumpet players. It came from pianist and composer Jonny King's *An Insider's Guide to Understanding and Listening to Jazz* (1997, Walker). After talking about other of the jazz instruments, on pages 61-62 he tackles the trumpet. Here is part of what he had to say.

The Egomaniacal Trumpet Player

Among musicians, trumpet players are reputed to have the biggest egos. As the other musicians see it, they're the cockiest guys on the bandstand. They... try to take over every tune and every gig and musical situation. Of course, such sweeping generalizations couldn't possibly be true for all trumpet players, but the trumpeter's reputation might be justified to a certain extent. You probably have to be somewhat brash to think that you can lead a quintet or power a big band's brass section with a pint-sized horn with only three valves....

Well, yes. That is our reputation, but at least he has the insight to see where some of it comes from- a pint-sized horn that powers a whole band. He goes on to give us some pretty heavy support:

The technique of playing the trumpet is bewildering to the rest of us. The horn is a small curved piece of brass (or other, more exotic metal finishes) with a mouthpiece the musician blows into and a "bell" that fans out from the horn and projects notes and sounds. The mouthpiece is a small metal cylinder into which the trumpeter must blow his tightened, purse lips. ... The trumpet is an extremely physically demanding instrument, and you can't lay off for more than a few days without seriously compromising your chops.

I had never thought about it that way. I started playing in 1961 at age 13. I don't remember any of the early fights with learning or how awful it must have sounded to my parents. And that bit about compromising your "chops" is one of the more famous issues to a trumpet player. Yeah. Wow. He understands.

Once you get a full head of steam and force air into the horn to create notes, how do you determine the pitches of those tones? By combining different amounts of air pressure, changing lip positions, and pressing down different combinations of the three valves, the trumpet is able to sound about three octaves worth of pitches. Most people are fairly blown away by the prospect of trying to control dozens of different notes with barely perceptible changes in lip positions and valve alterations.

As I was writing this, I was listening to Lee Morgan do everything described in that last paragraph- and then some- on the amazing "Just One of Those Things". He made it sound so smooth and easy- using only those barely perceptible lip changes and valve combinations.

When I initially read that description, I did react with surprise. After a while you just pick up the horn and start playing. It becomes second nature. It is natural and you don't think about why and how you do what you do. To describe it as King does gives a whole new dimension to what we do.

But, and this is important, I think, when we get that nonchalant or even carefree about our playing, we can find ourselves at a loss. That may have been the underlying secret insight I got a year ago at Shell Lake. In a brief moment of instruction from Bob Baca my whole way of looking at what I was doing as a musician changed. I know now that part of what happened was to take what had become natural and allow it to grow and change. When we are satisfied with how we are playing, we can get stuck and not move on.

For years I had been somewhat satisfied. I believed that perhaps this was as far as I could ever get. I was wrong. I am grateful I was wrong. I also found that it takes patience and persistence to move on to new levels. The suggestion that I could have a daily routine of long tones, chromatics, and scales brought me back to basics. In playing those long tones I have to listen, not just blow them. I have to hear the chromatics move. I have to be aware of the steps and half-steps of the scales. Yes, I am memorizing the scales; I am become familiar with the shape and movement of the sounds. But I don't just rattle them off so I can get on to something else.

THAT was a whole new understanding of practice and the road to improvement. It has worked- and for that I am grateful. And, yes, it does lead to second-nature playing because these routines and exercises become deeply ingrained in my brain and neural wiring. It is my whole musical self-learning, melding, and growing together.

That's how we learn and grow in anything important. But we can never be lackadaisical about it. All these are gifts. Yet if we don't use them and improve them, we can get stuck. I like where music has taken me. I can hardly wait to see what's next.

Chapter 2.2

The Way You Do Everything

In one of our discussions at the trumpet workshop it was pointed out that many of us would not be making a living as a musician. As much as we love playing trumpet, that will not be our "day job." In the different bands I play in a majority of the members are not professional musicians. Health care and computers have both been a major part of the community's economic base. As a result there are many different health care professionals and computer engineers in the groups. Sure, there are also a sizable number of band and music teachers as well as some who make their living performing music.

As we thought about this, we were reminded of something that we should not forget.

> Things you learn playing the trumpet will make you a better… surgeon, teacher, worker, friend, spouse, etc.

We all have various skills and personalities. What we discover in playing music- the discipline, the ability to work with others- are also essential to our vocations. What music teaches us is very much what is essential in our lives.

It's also a two-way street: If you have developed into a good (fill in the blank), you can become a good musician. It takes the same commitment, discipline, and work. The things you learn in life or career will make you a better trumpet player.

This brought to mind a comment a friend made to me back in July. He was talking about some of the wisdom he has been given by others and quoted this tidbit. It boggled my mind and twisted my life like very few things do:

The way you do anything is the way you do everything.

Looking it up on Google I found that there are a number of apparent "sources" for it. In any case, it is one of those statements that is so profound as to shift one's world view.

- Do you find shortcuts at work in order to get done faster, although not necessarily more effectively? That may very well be how you do a lot of other things?
- Do you treat people with condescension and not really care about them? Chances are that's how you treat your family and friends as well as strangers.
- Are you careless in how you take care of things you own? Are you taking care of even important things in the same way?
- Are you satisfied with "good enough" in projects you work on? Maybe "good enough" is all that you will ever be able to achieve.

This is not meant as a judgement but an observation. If we don't pay attention to how we do some things, chances are we may find it hard to pay attention to other things. This has to do with style and habit as much as with a conscious attempt on our part. It has to do with what we want to get out of our day-to-day lives and how much we put into it. It does not mean suddenly becoming a Type-A workaholic. It does not mean that we change our entire way of doing things. Some of us are more intuitive and introverted while others of us are far more cautious about making sure we plan well. Some of us would die if our entire day was closely scheduled while others would die if it wasn't. It is rather about how we utilize who we are, our personalities, skills, etc. in order to reach our goals.

Two weeks ago, I was talking with this friend again and told him about how he had thrown me into a mental wrestling match. He agreed that the same had happened to him. It was then I realized that his statement along with the discussion at camp had been at work for me in this past year. For over 18 months I have been working on what it means to be retired. Yes, I am still working part-time, but I have been wandering around being retired. That has given me to be able to develop what I have called my "third-career." While I did expand my music into a nearly full-time avocation, I knew there was more to it.

Then a year ago, the events that started this Tuning Slide blog threw me into a completely new way of working on my music. Within a few months I went from a person who worked on whatever needed working on to a systematic trumpet player. After nine months of increased practice at a 7 out of 10-day pattern I made it to the daily practice level. Since mid-April, for example, I have missed two days of playing my trumpet- both long travel days. My trumpet playing is probably the best it's ever been. [By the end of year two, I will be averaging 9 days out of 10. Quite a change!]

But the real surprise I realized two weeks ago, after a year of a whole new regimen of music practice, discipline, and growth, a number of things came together in June and July. It was a true "A-Ha" moment as it all made sense. Some of my retirement questions seemed to disappear and I found the direction I have been waiting for. In other words, the way I was doing music in new ways, was the way I was now doing some new things with my retirement.

The way you do anything, is the way you do everything. It can go from the music to other things- or from other things to the music. In reality it is not an either-or idea. It is a both-and action. It doesn't even have to be conscious. When you discover a new path, a new idea, a new discipline, a new reason for getting out of bed in the morning- that will interact with everything you have been doing.

How then do we do that? How do we work at making sure we are doing our "everything" the right way to be healthy and helpful to us? How can we aim at living a life that is consistent, starting with our musicianship?

First is passion. What excites you? What are you willing to take extra time to accomplish?

Second is focus. Are you ready to bear down and discover what living out that passion means? Are you honest with yourself about what that will mean- what sacrifices you will have to make, what changes you will have to work on- in order to be successful?

If what you say you are passionate about doesn't move you to do, can you really say it is a passion? This takes dedication and determination. It takes a commitment to do- not just talk.

Make your list. Begin to think about some goals. Look at ways you can enhance and grow from your previous experiences and efforts.

Now, how does this apply to the everyday things that you do- simple things like how you follow through with promises, how you treat your family and friends, your simple actions? Do these fall in line with what you have written- or do they show that you need to do some changing in order to get where you are going?

It takes that kind of commitment. In the Twelve-Step recovery programs there is an often-used question based on a phrase from the Alcoholics Anonymous Big Book:

> If you have decided you want what we have and are willing to go to any lengths to get it....

If you have decided you want to move into the area of your passion- or even just to be better at being who you are as a person, are you willing to go to whatever lengths are needed to get there?

Don't worry. We don't have to do it overnight.

So, get out that horn and keep working. The way you do your music is the way you do everything.

Chapter 2.3

No Small Parts

Many of us have no doubt made the statement: It's only a small part. It's just the 4th trumpet.

As a result, many of us have no doubt also heard a director make the statement: There are no small parts; only small players.

That's a hard thing to keep in mind sometimes when you have been an almost professional 3rd or 4th trumpet. You play your part and wonder longingly at the soaring lines of the first or the intricate solos the second develops. Every now and then your part has some interesting counterpoint or even a kind of fun note in a chord. But most of the time it's just that "small" part. Historically, in many high schools and even college bands, the less talented players were often placed at 3rd and 4th. The parts didn't go too high, they weren't all that technically difficult. As one progressed through high school, the older students would move up to 2nd and 1st places. It was as much seniority as skill at times, and could be overcome by a truly gifted musician. But, overall, people would covet those upper parts. So, in essence, they gave the seemingly "small" musicians the 3rd and 4th.

I used to say that I enjoyed playing 3rd or 4th since it meant that I didn't have to practice as much or develop the embouchure. I could just show up and play (sort of) and go home. But it also meant that I didn't have to practice anything difficult or challenging. Sure, you have to know how to count rests and syncopated notes from time to time. In general, though, it was an easy way out of getting better.

If you don't practice, if you don't challenge yourself, nothing happens.

In the past year of working through this Tuning Slide and my personal skill development, a couple of different things have happened.

First was when a local orchestra contacted me because they needed a 4th trumpet for one piece at the spring concert. Did I say that loudly enough? They **NEEDED** a 4th trumpet! No smart remarks, please, about why would anyone need a 4th trumpet? There is a very clear answer to that:

Because the composer wrote a 4th trumpet part! The composer/arranger wanted a 4th part.

I felt good about being able to do it, especially since the piece was a concert piece of selections from the great musical, Les Misérables. Overall, it was a typical 4th trumpet part. But it wasn't my typical 4th trumpet part. It had sections in all kinds of keys that we don't normally play very often- you know- 5 and 6 sharps (B major and F# major). I was glad that I had spent hours working on the 12 major scales last winter. It took some concentration, but the 5 and 6 sharps didn't send me into panic- although it did send me to the woodshed. It wasn't an "easy" or "small" part. Sometimes it doubled the 3rd, which is what the composer/arranger wanted. That note was obviously important. It needed a little more emphasis in tone, color, and location in the chord.

I think I am being clear about what I am trying to say:

All parts are important- that's why they were written in the first place!

That's the first thing that happened. It was an important lesson. The next thing was hearing the comment again at Shell Lake:

All parts are important. We had a trumpet choir of 50 musicians - and some of the arrangements had four, five, six parts. Wait a minute? Why all those extra parts? What is so important about those "lower" parts? Well, at first it was simple to say that it was because we only had trumpets and someone had to play those "lower" notes of the chords. With no horns, or trombones, or tuba- where was that foundation to come from. Other trumpets, obviously. Again, 4th, 5th, and 6th parts were needed. But it also brought to mind that when there are six parts, there is a reason that there are six parts. All the parts are pieces of the whole. Hmmmm.

"Pay attention, Barry," was the message I was getting from all of this. As my skills and range have increased, that does not mean I can - or should - leave the 3rd and 4th behind.

All parts are important- that's why they were written in the first place!

So I decided to try something in the big band I have played in for the past 8 years- the big band where I am the eternal 4th trumpet. When I started in the group my admitted skills for the group were more important in the range of being the announcer than of being a trumpet player. I needed to learn the language of the big band and playing jazz. Years of listening needed to be translated into being able to speak the language and not just listen. Playing 4th allowed me a lot of leeway to do that- and it allowed me to develop the announcing for the band as a part of the entertainment. But after all these years now, it was feeling boring. (A dangerous word. It can lead to stupid decisions and bad actions. Stay away from boredom!) But wait a minute. I was now playing with more confidence, better tone, and (mostly) able to speak the language.

If there are no small parts, why not see what it feels like to play the 4th part as if it was important and not just added on to give me, the announcer, something to do between announcements?

The first evening I really had the chance to try that out in any serious way was this past week in rehearsal. We were working on some more difficult pieces- both in intensity and sound. Chords were all over the place giving different tone and color to the piece. There was one point where over several measures a tension was built and released through a series of half and whole notes in the trumpet section. The first time we played it, something didn't feel right. My ear said that we were off somehow or another. I glanced at the person who was "leading" us at the time and it looked like he heard it, too. It was not a dissonance that was written into the score. It just was wrong.

Without saying anything about it we tried it again. This time as we came to that section, I consciously paid closer attention to what I was playing, hitting each of the notes more clearly- solid and centered. It sounded right. It fit. When we were done the leader made the comment that the difference he heard was that I played that 4th part with the strength it needed in order to be the foundation for the sound of the section. I don't know if anyone else did anything different that time. I just know I did- and it made a difference.

All parts are important- that's why they were written in the first place!

Now, would anyone in an audience ever noticed that there was something out of sync the first time we played it? Probably few if any would have. Would they have noticed the difference the second time? On some level, perhaps. My guess is that there would have been some emotional reaction they had that was more positive the second time. That's often the level at which these things make a difference. So why worry? Why make a big deal about it?

For one, because in the long run it is the accumulation of those seemingly small things that make the difference for better or worse. Playing a whole number where there are a series of "off" moments will certainly reduce the positive impact on the audience- and, of course, vice versa. We want the audience to have the best experience possible. That's the issue of "sound" and "tone" that is essential to music which we will talk about in coming posts.

Just as importantly, though, we make a big deal about it because it helps make us better musicians and keeps us connected to the integrity of the song itself. We are being true to the music and to who we are as musicians and people. That intentionality then expands in our lives to other things we do. We become more conscious of the way we treat others, the way we do our job, the way we respond to issues and concerns.

In life, as in music, there are no small parts!

(Sidenotes: 1) The orchestra called me again for the fall concert as 4th parts were again needed. 2) I am looking forward to the next year of more intentionally being the 4th trumpet in the big bands. Let's see what else I can learn.)

Chapter 2.4

What's Number 1?

Why do we do what we do as musicians?

Somewhere at some time in the past- distant for some, more recent for others- music made us stop and pay attention. Most likely it happened when we heard something in music and our world changed.

Mine was in junior high music class. The teacher told us to listen to his piece of music and tell what we hear. The needle dropped and I heard cars and people and the noise of a city through a series of notes and instrumentation that I later learned were iconic. When a few moments passed she stopped and asked us what we heard. I tended to be shy and didn't raise my hand in class very much at that point so I remained silent.

She looked around the room. I don't remember if anyone else said anything. I do remember her telling us the name of the piece.

An American in Paris by George Gershwin. I had heard correctly. The music was alive and real.

Several years earlier I had taken piano lessons for a year but had never stayed with it. I liked making music, or at least trying to. But I wasn't hooked.

Around the same time as the American in Paris experience I started playing trumpet after much badgering of parents who expected it would be a repeat of the piano. Fortunately, it wasn't. Again, because something happened. I don't know what it was in this instance. I do know that music became a central part of my life. It was September 1961, 55 years ago. Music is even more central today than it ever was- both listening and playing.

As a performing musician of various skill levels and involvement over these 55 years I can honestly say I have never wanted to quit. There were fallow periods when I didn't play much if at all. But it was never far away. My brain kept yearning, even if it was just at Christmas and Easter, or singing along with the radio.

Music is always number one!

Maria Popova wrote about this aspect of music for performing musicians on her web site, Brain Pickings. (https://www.brainpickings.org/2015/01/29/music-brain-ted-ed/)

> *"Each note rubs the others just right, and the instrument shivers with delight. The feeling is unmistakable, intoxicating,"* musician Glenn Kurtz wrote in his sublime meditation on the pleasures of practicing, adding: *"My attention warms and sharpens… Making music changes my body."* Kurtz's experience, it turns out, is more than mere lyricism — music does change the body's most important organ, and changes it more profoundly than any other intellectual, creative, or physical endeavor. (Kurtz, **Practicing: A Musician's Return to Music**)

Then, quoting TED-Ed author Anita Collins, Popova leads us to an insight about how powerful music playing is:

> Playing music is the brain's equivalent of a full-body workout… Playing an instrument engages practically every area of the brain at once — especially the visual, auditory, and motor cortices. And, as in any other workout, disciplined, structured practice in playing music strengthens those brain functions, allowing us to apply that strength to other activities… Playing music has been found to increase the volume

and activity in the brain's corpus callosum — the bridge between the two hemispheres — allowing messages to get across the brain faster and through more diverse routes. This may allow musicians to solve problems more effectively and creatively, in both academic and social settings.

My guess is that at that somewhere moment in time our brains were filled with neurotransmitters and emotions and our mid-brain knew that it was good! Even when it got boring, we kept at it because it has been good and we knew it. The more we worked at it, the more we practiced, the stronger our brains became (that full-body workout of the brain!). It is dangerous to say, but in that our brain was hijacked. We can never be the same again.

That's what got us going- and even keeps us going. It sounds like making music, then is all about us- the musician. And not anyone else. Just us. We do it to please ourselves. Which will get us nowhere. One of those seemingly insignificant statements that float about the room at the Shell Lake Trumpet Workshop points this out.

No matter what:

- The music is number one. It is first and foremost,
- Fellow musicians are second,
- The audience is third, and
- You are fourth.

Let's take a quick look at each and see how this fall into place.

The music is first.

The music has to be there and, let's be honest, it has to sound good. It has to have that element of the notes rubbing together that Kurtz is quoted as writing above. The instrument shivers with delight when all those things come together. We strive for that moment. We want that moment to happen every time we pick up our instrument, even when playing those seemingly endless long tones and scales. If Clarke #2 has never done that for you, try it next time you play it. That's what hooked us in the first place- the music.

Unlike a substance addiction where you can never get back to that first "high", with continuing practice and dedication you can go beyond that first musical hook to even greater heights and depths. The first time I played Clarke #2 starting on the high G at the top of the staff was a moment as fulfilling and exciting as when I first played "The Saints" 55 years ago. It is the music that perpetuates itself in us, fulfills us, and helps us move to the next stage of our performance ability. We want to make the music and we want to make better music.

Fellow musicians are second.

But we can't do it alone all the time. Music is a communal act. It is done with others. Even the greatest soloists in any musical genre cannot maintain a solo act with no supporting musicians. In saying that our fellow musicians we play with are second means that we are building a community of people working together to make music. The music lives when it involves others. The music lives when we make the music WITH others. The tone and color change; the rhythm can be different. Even if we are playing in unison, it is more than one person. Plus, as we have no doubt discovered many times, our part sounds different when played with the rest of the parts. Hitting that top of the staff F is a lot easier when it is in a major chord than when it is rubbing against some minor dis-chord.

The audience is third.

And yes, we have to play FOR someone else. I think I knew that way back in my early days. I would dream of planning and performing a concert for my family. What would be the order? What do I need to work on? What will please them? Some of that may have been a way of atoning for all the "bad" sounds they had to endure, but it was also a natural extension of the music's communal aspect. The music had a long way to go, but they seemed to enjoy what I did, if only because I was doing it for them. That group sitting out there in the auditorium or concert hall wants the music we have to offer. Bruce Springsteen was talking on TV the other night about the magic that happens in concert. The interaction between us and our audience is critical for good music. Sure, we can play exceptionally well without that feedback, but the chemistry of performers and audience is exciting and energizing.

I am fourth.

In other words, in the end it is not about me.

Yes, playing music moves us. Yes, playing music does all kinds of healthy things for us, the musicians. Yes, music makes us better people. But in the end, it is not about us. It is about #1- the music. The music does not primarily serve us and our needs as the musician.

- We serve the music.
- We support our fellow musicians.
- We present our offering of music to the audience.
- We are moved, filled, energized, and carried to further service.

Chapter 2.5

Finding the Center

How is it that this bunch of metal can make music? Whether I'm working on a Bach piece for the quintet or listening to Doc soar skyward from the very lowest G to far higher than I can go, this comes out of the same basic physics and metallurgy of the instrument we share in common. This is just as true for any instrument, but those of us who play wind instruments depend on some special properties of tubes. (Yes, that's really all a trumpet or sax or clarinet are- a long tube.) To understand some of the basics of our instrument, let's look at some physics. Don't worry, I'm not a physicist so it won't get too technical.

As with all brass instruments, sound is produced by blowing air through closed lips, [pushing air] into the mouthpiece and starting a standing wave vibration in the air column inside the trumpet. The player can select the pitch from a range of overtones or harmonics by changing the lip aperture and tension (known as the embouchure). (https://en.wikipedia.org/wiki/Trumpet)

Standing waves are produced. Waves have frequencies. They have "sound" when they are in a frequency range we can hear. Our famous western tuning note of A440 means that the frequency (distance from one top to the next top) of the standing wave is 440 Hz, or 440 cycles/second. Fortunately, the way sound waves work in a tube, for example, produces more than just the base frequency or wave. Otherwise, the sound would be dull and lacking in a lot of character. These other waves are known as overtones.

Simply put, these are various multiples of the original fundamental frequency of the wave. The higher the note, the fewer the overtones and the closer the next note. Overly simplified, I know. Don't worry about the specifics of the physics. If it works, we don't have to know how. There's one more bit of acoustics that explains the sound of our instruments. That is resonance.

Resonance is when one object vibrating at the same natural frequency of a second object forces that second object into vibrational motion. If you have two tuning forks, for example, and strike the one producing its frequency, the other tuning fork can then start vibrating in the same or related frequency.

These are the elements of what happens within the folds and valves of the trumpet. It is the ability of the sound to be reinforced or prolonged by reflection from the inner surfaces and setting them into their own vibrations. The result is that they is a deeper, fuller sound. It is how many overtones we are playing at a single moment. Lower notes tend to have greater resonance than higher notes because of the overtones, frequencies, tube length, etc. As we learn to play higher notes, we strengthen the resonance. That's why someone like Doc can hit those high notes and still produce resonance where mine sounds like a screeching baby bird being strangled.

Hold on, I'm just about through with the physics. It will all make sense even if you don't understand the full science.

One of the reasons that Doc or Maynard (or whoever your favorite trumpet player is) can have a resonance in their higher register- as well as in their whole range- is that they have learned to keep the sound centered. The center of the horn, the center of that lead pipe or tuning slide, is where the sound is most effectively and efficiently produced. It allows the standing wave to go right down the middle and its overtones to be centered with it. Get it off-center and the sound deteriorates. Quickly.

In the end the center of the horn is where the resonance is. Therefore, in order to get the rich, full sound, all you have to do is find the center and play into it. Center the tone; center the air; you will improve your sound. That explains the simple exercise of "playing the lead pipe." You can hear the centering happen.

How do you learn to do that? In looking at this basic explanation of trumpet acoustics, we have reached the very basics of trumpet practice and development- finding ways to center our sound. Since it is basic, it should come as no surprise that it is...

Long tones!

Yep, those boring exercises in holding a note for an "extended" period of time are probably the most important thing we will ever learn about being a trumpet player. It looks like, from an acoustics and metallurgical standpoint, everything else builds on top of that. You don't have to know the science, but it helps me visualize what is important when I am doing long tones. And in visualization, we are actually helping ourselves to do what we are wanting to do.

When you play those long tones, it may be helpful to picture in your mind the sound wave moving down the lead pipe. As it does make sure it stays in the center in your mind's eye. Through the wonders of the nerves and workings of our brain that actually helps us to guide the air that way in the world of the trumpet itself. We often overlook the mind-body connections and the power of visualization and thought.

Well, how long should we play a given long tone. There are all kinds of advice on the Internet about how long, in time, "long" is. Some say hold it for as long as you can keep it centered and steady. Others talk about a flowing series of long tones. Look up Schlossberg #6 at Greg Wing Trumpet for a really helpful exercise of long tones. (http://www.gregwingtrumpet.com/uploads/2/1/4/0/21407028/schlossberg_6.pdf)

In general, though, here are four definitions of what is long enough:

- Long enough to keep it centered

  When we are first warming up the sound will not be as centered as it can be. For those of us who are less advanced, such centeredness comes with time. But you will hear the difference.

  Long enough to hold it steady

Once we hear it getting centered the next step is to keep it steady there. That means the force behind the breath and the abdominal support.

- Long enough to hold the dynamics.

Pick a dynamic and hold it. Many recommendations are to play it soft, then next time softer, holding it at the pianissimo level for the duration.

- Long enough to listen! Really listen!

Can you hear it? No? Then do it again. Hold and listen. Keep the breath and dynamic steady.

One very useful way to get started is just playing the "tube" the lead pipe. Take the tuning slide out and play 2nd line "G". Listen for the centeredness, the steadiness. Listen again. Do it regularly at the start of your practice and you will be ready for the notes that come next.

Long tones can be a good 10-minute warm-up. Not strenuous, but solid. As perfect a way to get your session going as any.

Bruce Chidester on The Trumpet Blog has a list of 10 reasons to do long tones. Here are four of them:

- Long tones give you the opportunity to listen to your sound- by listening to your sound; there is a natural tendency to improve on what you are listening to.
- Long tones help you analyze what is going on within your air stream. Opening and closing the channel which encompasses the passage of air will dictate the timbre of your tone.
- Long tones train your arms and hands to support the instrument more steadily for any shaking in these areas will telegraph into a shaky tone.

- Long tones are the direct opposite of fast, highly technical passages and thus need to be implemented to balance your technical playing.

(http://www.thetrumpetblog.com/long-tones-10-reason-to-do-them/)

But there's another piece of being centered. It fits in with the principle that the way you do is how you do everything. Being "centered" in ourselves may be the most important thing we can do for our health and daily living. It gives us a place to go to within ourselves when stress gets overwhelming. It gives us a way to gather our thoughts and focus ourselves. What we are talking about above with "centering" the sound is a form of focusing the sound. It increases our ability at mindful attention to what is happening. It trains our brains to control our body to produce the sound we want. Apply that now to who you are.

You- the musician- need to be able to be centered in yourself. You need to sense and enhance the resonance that happens around you and within you. That rich, vibrant sense of life alive can enhance all that you do.

That means attention to breathing. That means attention to how we are feeling and reacting to our surroundings. That means being aware of the physical tensions and tightness that so easily derails us. That is one important piece of my own personal work. I have learned a lot of that mindfulness and breathing in so many areas of my life. Now I am applying it to my trumpet playing. My performance anxiety, for example, can be eased with self-centering. My listening for the centering of my sound in long tones teaches me what being centered feels like. It relaxes my muscles and I find I am playing with a more relaxed tone. If we do not play "centered" we can find ourselves playing "tight", constricting the sound. Playing tight also tires me out more quickly because my breath isn't centered or easily flowing. It is a wondrous cycle of the flow of our lives.

Seek the resonance within you- and in your music.

Chapter 2.6

All About the Sound

Last week I talked about the basic (and oversimplified) physics and acoustics of trumpet playing. Being centered in sound was at the heart of it and the way practicing long tones can help us visualize and enhance the resonance of the sound we produce. That can then lead us to finding ways to center our own lives through focus, visualization, and breathing. The result is the congruence of who we are and how we play.

Now I want to look a little more at this fine instrument many of us have fallen in love (and hate?) with. First, here's how it's made from the How Products Are Made website:

> Brass instruments are almost universally made from brass, but a solid gold or silver trumpet might be created for special occasions. The most common type of brass used is yellow brass, which is 70 percent copper and 30 percent zinc. Other types include gold brass (80 percent copper and 20 percent zinc), and silver brass (made from copper, zinc, and nickel). The relatively small amount of zinc present in the alloy is necessary to make brass that is workable when cold. Some small

manufacturers will use such special brasses as Ambronze (85 percent copper, 2 percent tin, and 13 percent zinc) for making certain parts of the trumpet (such as the bell) because such alloys produce a sonorous, ringing sound when struck. Some manufacturers will silver- or gold-plate the basic brass instrument.

Very little of the trumpet is not made of brass. Any screws are usually steel; the water key is usually lined with cork; the rubbing surfaces in the valves and slides might be electroplated with chromium or a stainless nickel alloy such as monel; the valves may be lined with felt; and the valve keys may be decorated with mother-of-pearl. (http://www. madehow.com/Volume-1/Trumpet.html)

[Not a surprise that they look for alloys that produce a "sonorous, ringing sound." That's part of the overall acoustics we talked about last week. The trumpet is about $5.00 or so in metal. Probably less on the junk market where you may get as much as $1.30/pound. Weighing in at an average 2.5 pounds of metal, you might get $3 - $3.50 for the metal as junk. The thousands of dollars a Strad costs is in the design that helps make the sound.] Back to How It's Made:

The most important feature of a trumpet is sound quality. Besides meeting exacting tolerances of approximately 1×105 meters, every trumpet that is manufactured is tested by professional musicians who check the tone and pitch of the instrument while listening to see if it is in tune within its desired dynamic range. The musicians test-play in different acoustical set-ups, ranging from small studios to large concert halls, depending on the eventual use of the trumpet. Large trumpet manufacturers hire professional musicians as full-time testers, while small manufacturers rely on themselves or the customer to test their product.

Now comes what may be the most important paragraph from the website:

At least half the work involved in creating and maintaining a clear-sounding trumpet is done **by the customer**. [Emphasis added.] The delicate instruments require special handling, and, because of their inherent asymmetry, they are prone to imbalance. Therefore, great care must be taken so as not to carelessly damage the instrument. To prevent dents, trumpets are kept in cases, where they are held in place by trumpet-shaped cavities that are lined with velvet. The trumpet needs to be lubricated once a day or whenever it is played. The lubricant is usually a petroleum derivative similar to kerosene for inside the valves, mineral oil for the key mechanism, and axle grease for the slides. The grime in the mouthpiece and main pipe should be cleaned every month, and every three months the entire trumpet should soak in soapy water for 15 minutes. It should then be scrubbed throughout with special small brushes, rinsed, and dried.

Perhaps I am overdoing it with this whole thing, but the one thread working through these quotes as well as what we talked about last week:

The Sound.

It's all about the sound! Sound is everything- tone, upper register, melody, etc.

Everything is done in order to produce the best sound possible. From the chemistry of mixing metals to the long tones we practice, the end product is the best sound possible from the instrument you own. Period. With that in mind let me quote Mr. Bob Baca from the Shell Lake Trumpet Workshop.

These are the three characteristics of a **great** trumpet player:

1. Every time you play you have a **great**- not a good- sound.
2. You have **great**- not good- rhythm.
3. You have **great**- not good- ears to hear the sound.

Let's expand some more about developing a great sound. Remember that after the right mix of metals, tubing, etc. it is:

- being centered,
- finding the resonance,

- utilizing long tones in our basic practice.

Going beyond those basics. here are some thoughts from Brass Musician magazine's web site a couple years ago.

> We must have a very definite concept of a beautiful tone in order to produce a great sound. Conception of tone is a mental memory, aural visualization, imagination or recollection of what a beautiful tone sounds like. We cannot imagine or remember what we have not heard and memorized so we must frequently listen to fine players live and on recordings. Daily listening to recordings of fine players will develop our concept of tone. ... Playing along with recordings... helps imprint the aural role model and imitation in our minds.

Olympic champion Michael Phelps and Duke basketball coach Mike Krzyzewski were interviewed on TV. Both of them spoke of the value of "visualization." Phelps said he works through the possibilities in a race beforehand- including potential problems. That way, he said, he will be ready for anything. Coach K. said he prepares visualizations for his players to use on iPads. They can see what a "champion" looks like- how champions carry themselves- including how they walk and talk. That's what the above paragraph is talking about. You can't hit the notes if you don't know what they sound like. What better way to learn than to hear them, get them aurally imprinted, visualize the sound, and then "rehearse" it in your mind. I have heard a number of musicians say they hear the note or sound in that small fraction of a second before they play it.

For years I had the problem of not being able to come in on the right note after a rest, or at the beginning of a piece. Sometimes the note would slide off downward or I would overshoot it higher. It was particularly difficult if it was happening during or after an unusual chord structure where my note didn't seem to be right. I asked one of my colleagues how she did it- and why I was having difficulty. She simply told me that I have to hear the note before I play it. No, I do not have anything like perfect or near-perfect pitch. If you asked me to sing that note in tune I probably couldn't. What I could do was take a second and silently "sing" my way to the note using the open tones- middle C, G, and the C on the staff. That helped with the B or D on the staff. If I was going for the E or F at the top of the staff, I just silently sang the open notes to the E. It worked. I am still not in the habit of doing that as regularly as I could, but I don't miss the notes as often as I used to.

Such visualization helps with a player like me who tends to be somewhat lazy in hitting notes. It focuses, centers my sound and keeps me in the music. That also means I am less tense when I come to the notes. I find myself able to hit the note with a stronger sound, probably more in tune and less pressured. Which brings me to the next paragraph from Brass Musician:

> A steady relaxed airstream is critical to a full, beautiful tone. … When we ascend into the upper register we should blow faster and avoid tightening the abdominal muscles, which restricts the throat and causes a strained, brighter, sharper sound. There are many ways to improve breathing, blowing and tone. I recommend visiting windsong-press.com, reading books and articles about or by Arnold Jacobs…

- Steady
- Relaxed
- Don't tighten the abs
- Keep the throat open

Seems simple enough. Check your shoulder position? Have you pulled your shoulders up toward your ears? You are probably tense. Drop them. Let them droop. Are you holding the trumpet with a left-hand death grip? Relax. That tension is going all the way up your arm and even into your jaw. Loosen it. It is amazing how much physical work is involved in playing a trumpet. For me it even goes to my posture either sitting or standing. I know, sadly, that if I took the iconic "Miles Davis Stance" I would not be relaxed. MY sound, at least at this point, would be constricted. That may be part of what Miles wanted. For me, it hurts my style. I have to sit up, give my abs the room to relax. Leaning forward tightens them, reduces my airflow and abdominal support for my sound.

That is where those infernal long tones help. Playing them in a relaxed but appropriate position helps our bodies to learn how to do it and enhance our muscle memory.

Arnold Jacobs is mentioned above. He was principal tubist for the Chicago Symphony and many consider Jacobs one of the great music instructors of the second half of the 20th Century. He has become well known as an expert on breathing and wind instruments.

(Here is a collection of quotes and explanations of some of what he taught. http://blog.davidtuba.com/en/brass/10-quotes-musicians-arnold-jacobs-i)

One of the quotes and explanations from the above site. (Bold in original):

> **"Conceive, don't perceive"**
> **Controlling our thoughts** is one of the **most important parts of musical performance**. When we are playing, it is very common to ask ourselves questions like "does this sound good?" "am I breathing right?", "am I using my fingers correctly", "do I feel okay?", etc.
>
> Arnold Jacobs thinks **we shouldn't ask ourselves these kind of questions during the performance** because we're sending information from our muscles to our brain when we should be doing exactly the opposite; **creating music in our mind and making our muscles to produce it**.
>
> As Jacobs says, **"be a great artist in your imagination"**, since **analysis does not help performance.** If we want to progress and improve, we should present what we want listeners to perceive.
>
> Jacobs points out that musicians **should show their feeling and tell stories with their sound.** If we want a specific color in our sound, we have to create it in our mind and then our body will produce it by making the necessary adjustments. **The idea is to tell a story though musical order.**

All this talk about breathing- remember that it is always in support of the sound, the great sound that we should always be seeking for. Breathing is the best way to start in any attempt to improve our playing. But it is also the starting point for stress reduction, personal centering, meditative focus, and many other introductions to better health.

Keep breathing- and learning to breathe better.

Chapter 2.7

Feel the Rhythm

Last week I quoted one of the ideas from this past summer's Shell Lake Trumpet workshop:

There are three characteristics of a **great** trumpet player:

1. Every time you play you have a **great**- not a good- sound.
2. You have **great**- not good- rhythm.
3. You have **great**- not good- ears to hear the sound.

This week we focus on rhythm.

"Life is about rhythm. We vibrate, our hearts are pumping blood, we are a rhythm machine, that's what we are."

—Mickey Hart (percussionist, Grateful Dead)

Pulse.

Heartbeat.

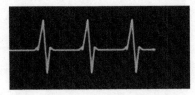

For us, we start with this simple definition:

Rhythm is the arrangement of sounds as they move through time. (http://www.rhythm-in-music.com/introduction-what-is-rhythm-definition.html)

We know the synonyms. They are common in our musical language:

Beat.

Tempo.

Cadence.

We are not just talking about the groove though. Groove is a basic part of rhythm, but it goes beyond that. Rhythm is not just what a "rhythm section" does. What IS rhythm? I asked Bob Baca, our Trumpet Workshop director for his thought. (His comments in italics.):

> *Rhythm is the underlying pulse that creates initial emotion far greater than color or attack can achieve. All music, including cadenza must have an underlying pulse. In Western European Classical Music that pulse is some sort of a duple or triple subdivision. In classical music, although solid tone is of first importance, conscious rhythm is a close second.*

That's a good start. Rhythm is not just the beat; it is one of the ways that music creates emotion. All the standards we think of in music- crescendos and decrescendos, tension and release, accents and slurs, major and minor chords- are part of the rhythm of the music. That brings the music to life. Without those elements, a straight, non-changing sound would put us to sleep. Just plodding along at a steady level allows not tension and interest. Using only one chord without variation would get dull.

That is rhythm. What does it mean, though, to have great rhythm? Back to Bob Baca for a very simple answer.

Conscious Rhythm. We want to feel but not hear rhythm.

From the perspective of the listener, a song with great rhythm is not what you hear, but what you feel. It is what makes you move in response to what is being played. It can be overpowering to our senses if the rhythm is forced into the forefront. Sure- a good drum and rhythm section solo can be fun, but not for a whole song. Watch a Buddy Rich video, for example, and you will see conscious rhythm at work- and Rich doesn't even look like he's doing anything. You watch him and you feel the rhythm as all the other instruments play. Just Buddy playing, dull after awhile. The band without Buddy, if not dull, probably chaos. Together- the rhythm works.

From the perspective of the musician, rhythm is what we find when we move beyond simply playing the notes and trying to get them right. We move to playing the right notes, at the right time, in the right place, in the right way. The right way being in the rhythm of the song.

Rhythm can be easy to lose, of course. We've all heard a band or group get "out of rhythm" for any one of a number of reasons. Sometimes it is difficulty in communication across the group. Sometimes someone wants to jump in too early or misses the beat too late. (That is way too often me!) That's where being conscious of rhythm is most needed.

Actually, if you think about it, rhythm is part of the language we are trying to learn. In jazz the way eighth notes swing is a piece of the language-rhythm. The feel of a Sousa march is a piece of the march language- rhythm. Feel the pace and pulse of a Bach chorale- that is a piece of the language of the music- rhythm.

Part of our work then is always in the fundamentals. As Bob Baca explained:

> *Where rhythm is most lost is usually at the ends of phrases, especially if the phrase ends with a long note. If a note is held full value, the rest in-between phrases become part of the rhythm and sounds musical.*

In our fundamentals we learn how to phrase our music. We learn the importance of "playing the rests" as much as playing the notes. Rests are essential to the rhythm; they help set the tension and release, they help give movement to the notes.

As I was writing this, an a cappella choral version of Amazing Grace came on my iTunes shuffle. Not a drum within hearing. I can imagine a conductor moving his arms in tempo, but beyond that it was all done by voice. Every rhythmic impulse of the song built through the melody line, the droning vocal bass accompaniment rising and falling. What was I doing? I was moving with the music. Not just because I know the song so well, but because the singers kept the rhythm alive. It had a living pulse.

So how do you get it? Said Mr. Baca:

Always have a legato subdivision in your head.

It seems that audio visualization is never far from our thinking and playing. How do you hear it before you play it? What I have found is that just picking up the trumpet and playing the notes is not often a helpful first step in learning the rhythm. Several instructors have talked often about

1. Reading the piece
2. Singing the piece
3. Listening to a recording of the piece.
4. Maybe repeating the process a time or two, and then
5. Pick up the instrument and play.

I am not sure that anyone has a natural ability to know and feel rhythm from a printed page. These steps of practice and learning help focus us to feel it, then hear it, then play it. Yet we are naturals at rhythm. We are born with it. We hear it in the beating of our mother's heart while in the womb. We hear the tide-like rush of blood traveling through her system. It is the original music.

In full harmony with the overall theme of this blog- reflections on life and music- Mr. Baca had one more thought:

Life is about rhythm.
The very earth that we live, rotates runs in a steady rhythm and music, our most positive expression of who we are, must as well.

Music, as Mr. Baca says, is the most positive expression of who we are. Throughout history people have made music. Throughout history music has started with rhythm. That rhythm is the heartbeat of life itself. Whether the sound of ocean tides or the "lub-dub" of the human heart, it underlies everything around us. It may even be that the very idea of sound- frequency, etc.- is a rhythm itself. What we do in our lives is find our place in that rhythm.

Again, from author and Grateful Dead drummer Mickey Hart.

In the beginning, there was noise. Noise begat rhythm, and rhythm begat everything else.

We are part of the physical expression of that rhythm. Translate it, hear it in your music, share it with others in your actions, make music! Philosopher Lao Tzu said once that the music of the soul can be heard by the universe.

Stop and listen for a moment and it may also be that the soul will hear the music of the universe.

Chapter 2.8

Listen to Grow

The past two weeks I looked at the first two parts of this statement from Shell Lake Trumpet Workshop

Three characteristics of a **great** trumpet player:

1. Every time you play you have a **great**- not a good- sound.
2. You have **great**- not good- rhythm.
3. You have **great**- not good- ears to hear the sound.

How does "great ears" add to this trio of greatness? What the heck does that even mean?

My first thought went to "ears" as the ability to be in a group and hear what others are doing. That would be the skill of blending your sound with the sound of the whole group. Not as easy a task as we might think. I am still amazed when one of my colleagues in the concert band knows when I have hit an F instead of an F#. (One of my most common errors.) Even when I wasn't playing loudly and they were sitting two chairs away from me. They have a good ear, perhaps even a great one. They know when my note isn't fitting into theirs. I can do that sometimes with others in the section, but it hasn't come easy.

Most of the time I am way too involved in myself to hear what the rest of the band is doing. I want to make sure that my "ears" hear "me." Fortunately, this has gotten better over the years. One of the best ways to work on it is to play in a smaller ensemble like the brass quintet I play with. After the first run through of a piece when we do end up concentrating on our own parts, then it is time to let the ears do more work. How do I fit in with the group? Am I hearing the chords and my place in them? Am I overpowering the other parts, throwing things out of balance? When there are only five of you and obviously only one on a part, these are not incidental questions. Thus one of the important pieces of having "great ears" is to know how to play well with others.

But I also realize that a lot of this has to do with what we do *before* we get into the rehearsal. As always it is found first in the practice rooms. Wondering how others understood this I asked Matt Stock, one of the faculty from Shell Lake Trumpet Workshop, to reflect on what "great ears" meant. He responded:

> I'm realizing more and more that "ears" is misleading. Generally, we think of that as just pitch or passing an aural skills test in school. The better definition would be the ability to conceive every detail of a performance (pitch, tone, time, expressive details, etc.) from a written score. I suppose good ears would be the ability to do that with the music you normally encounter and great ears would be the ability to do that at sight with the unexpected/unfamiliar and for a classical player transpose at sight. For a jazz player I suppose that would be the ability to react to unexpected chord substitutions, transcribe, etc.

I didn't expect that. "Ears" is the ability to go beyond just sight-reading when you see a new score. It is the ability to "hear" that score even before you play it. I don't necessarily mean to look at a full score and hear all the parts. That takes years and probably more time than most of us have if we are not becoming conductors or music majors. But it does mean to look at my part and see where it goes, what it does, and how it does it. It means audio visualization like we have talked about before.

In many ways this took me back to the ongoing fundamental analogy that music is a language we learn to speak. When we develop an "ear" for a language we are on the way to learning the language. It means that when we read the language on the printed page, we can "hear" it and know what it means. Then it moves to being able to hear the language when spoken and be able to know what is being said. That starts with mentally translating as you listen. To do that is very slow and means we miss a great deal of what the other person is saying. Then it moves to where certain words and phrases are understood without translating. You then start to use those phrases appropriately without needing to translate into or from our native language. Eventually if we are to really learn the language, we have to do more than read and listen- we have to internalize it and then speak what we hear. To do that with our music takes us back into the practice room and playing it.

If we have the opportunity, we need to hear it being played, of course. We have talked about listening to recordings of performances, then singing it, before playing a piece. That's hard to do in the middle of a rehearsal when a new piece is handed out or in the middle of improvising when an odd chord comes up. So we develop our ears to know what it sounds like before we play it- or to know what's happening when we hear it.

Back to playing in ensembles, that, too, is more than just hearing the others play. It is about the ability to hear when I am wrong. It is back to "ears" that know my style isn't matching the style of the lead trumpet, or that when I have a part that is a duet with the horn or trombone, that we have to be able to blend our sounds together. When we do that we change- and enliven- the color of the music. Playing in the quintet has been the single best way for me to develop my "ears." It still takes the practice room where I learn the language of my part. It takes the practice room to begin to put those sounds in the right place.

Back to Matt's thoughts:

> What helped me be more demanding with my ear training has been to record myself singing. With the Tonal Energy app you can record yourself and use the tuner when you play it back. In the ear training classes I took you passed if you ended up somewhere near the right note no matter how sloppy everything was along the way. This forces

you to be much more honest. It's humbling at first but pays off if you stick with it a few weeks.

In the practice room, the "great ears" come from working on them. It can be ear training, long tones (them again!) learning the sound of arpeggios in each key, or recording yourself. You won't develop great ears if you don't use them. Intentionally. (By the way, I looked up the two resources Matt mentioned. The Tonal Energy app looks like a really good overall resource- a tuner that does more than tell you that you are out of tune. Trumpet Multimedia has some excellent information. Thanks, Matt!)

Beyond just hearing the sound and playing it appropriately, this is about mindfulness in all that we do. As I have gotten older and more aware of the importance of paying attention, the whole concept of mindfulness has grown in value. Being mindful is about being in the moment, knowing where and who you are and how you fit in with what's happening around you. One definition I found:

> a mental state achieved by focusing one's awareness on the present moment, while calmly acknowledging and accepting one's feelings, thoughts, and bodily sensations...

Even more to the point is the definition from Jon Kabat-Zinn, one of the key founders of the ideas of mindfulness:

> Mindfulness is awareness that arises through paying attention, on purpose, in the present moment, non-judgmentally. It's about knowing what is on your mind.

- Paying attention

Concentrate on what's happening and going on within you and around you.
Take time to more than smell the roses- see them and appreciate them.

- On purpose

  Not as an afterthought, but being committed to your growth and development.
  Make it part of your daily plan to be aware and mindful.
  Allow the world to amaze you at what is happening that you may have missed before.

- In the present moment

  The past is history, the future a mystery, stay in the now.
  Our fretting over the past or worrying about tomorrow is one of the biggest obstacles to growth.
  Notice the world in all its infinite wonder.

- Non-judgmentally

  Don't be hard on yourself, judging, and over critical.
  You are where you are. You may not be where you want to be.
  But only when you accept the here and now can you begin to move beyond it.

When we practice this in our music, we will discover it in the world around us.

When we practice this in our daily lives, we will find the wonderful sound of our music.

"Ears."

It is more than just hearing.

Chapter 2.9

The Best Practice

Let me start this week with a quote from the book, *Peak: Secrets from the New Science of Expertise* by Anders Ericsson and Robert Pool.

> The best among us do not occupy that perch because they were born with some innate talent but rather because they have developed their abilities through years of practice, taking advantage of the adaptability of the human body and brain. (Ericsson, p. 256)

"Heresy," you say. "What about the Mozarts of the world; child prodigies who just seem to be able to do whatever they do naturally?"

Ericsson tears that myth to pieces, as does Angela Duckworth in Grit: *The Power of Passion and Perseverance.* Research indicates that innate talent seems to be a lot scarcer than we want to admit. So why does the myth persist? We all can have a good excuse why we aren't THAT good at whatever we do. "I wasn't born with that talent." While there may be predisposed for certain kinds of activities, the determining factor of the highly expert in many fields has nothing to do with that. It has to do with practice.

Oh, that again!

Yep. Even with something as seemingly mysterious as extremely advanced ability, the answer is not mysterious at all. In fact, as has often been quoted, the simplest answer is usually the most likely to be true. The incredible secret to becoming an expert is good old practice, practice, practice. Doc and Maynard and Miles got to their heights through practice. Being in the right place at the right time can help you get discovered, but there may very well be people who are as good as any of these icons who never had the opportunity to "make it." One of the reasons is, of course, that it takes a lot of work (!!) to reach those levels. It also is because we are often satisfied to live in the "comfortable rut of homeostasis and never do the work that is required to get out of it. [We] live in the world of 'good enough.' (P. 47)

With this introduction in mind, here is a summary from a book review:

> Not all practicing is equal. Ericsson identifies three different types of practicing. The most basic type of practicing is naïve practice, the generic rather mediocre practicing that children muddle through as they go from piano lesson to piano lesson. They will not become star performers, nor do they intend to.
>
> A much more effective type of practice is what Ericsson calls *purposeful practice*. Purposeful practice is not simply repetition. Instead, it is characterized by well-defined, specific goals. Instead of just playing a piece over and over, purposeful practice would require the piano student to play the entire piece three times in a row with no mistakes. The guiding principle of purposeful practice is to take baby steps — a bunch of them that, little by little, helps you reach the goal.
>
> There are other characteristics that separate purposeful practice from naïve practice:
>
> • Purposeful practice is focused. Students must give it their full attention.
>
> • Purposeful practice involves feedback. Immediate, specific feedback on where students are falling short is vital.

- Purposeful practice requires leaving one's comfort zone. If students aren't pushing themselves beyond what is comfortable and familiar, they will not advance.

Purposeful practice is more effective than naïve practice. (http://www.summary.com/book-reviews/_/Peak-Secrets-from-the-New-Science-of-Expertise/)

Ericsson makes it clear that there are good things about "purposeful practice." It is possible to improve one's abilities with it. But he points out clearly that trying hard or pushing yourself to the limits is not enough. (P. 25) Back to the summary:

> But to truly become an expert requires an even higher level of practice: *Deliberate practice*. Deliberate practice also pushes people out of their comfort zone and involves feedback and focus. However, deliberate practice is different from purposeful practice because it is based on proven techniques developed by past experts. "Deliberate practice is purposeful practice that knows where it is going and how to get there," Ericsson writes.

What makes "deliberate practice" better than "purposeful practice"? One is that it benefits from a history of well-established and well-developed strategies and standards that produce high levels of performance. (Music training, by the way, is one of the prime examples of this!) Second is that it requires a teacher who can push and provide significant feedback. Ericsson calls it "purposeful" and "informed." (P. 98)

Ericsson then goes on to list the traits that characterize "deliberate practice."

- It develops skills that others have already figured out how to do and for which effective training techniques have been established.
- It takes place outside of one's comfort zone and requires the student to try things that are just beyond current abilities.
- It involves well-defined, specific goals, not some vague overall improvement.

- It is deliberate- it requires a person's full attention and conscious actions.
- It involves feedback and modification of efforts in response to the feedback.
- It produces and depends on effective mental representations.
- It almost always involves building or modifying previously acquired skills by focusing on particular aspects ad working to improve them specifically.

Deliberate practice works thanks to one very special attribute of the human brain- plasticity. It harnesses the adaptability of the human brain in response to mental and physical training.

There's a lot of information in this one post. I will spend the next couple posts expanding on these and adding some hopefully helpful examples of how this can work. I will also look at the ideas of grit as talked about in Angela Duckworth's book mentioned earlier. This whole concept I have been discovering over the past six months is nothing short of remarkable. It makes me excited to read it and think about what it means for me. It is also quite simple. Far, far from easy. But simple and straightforward. It has worked for many, and can have an impact on any of us.

Keys to effective practice are the same as the keys to effective living. That I will also explore. But for the next week, think about these ideas and reflect some on how your practice brings some of these ideas together and what needs to be improved.

Be serious, but in the end, I think we should also be careful that we don't take ourselves too seriously. That can result in being too hard on ourselves. Being serious about our music- taking it seriously- is essential. But if it's a drudgery, we won't get to where we can go.

Have fun. That is one of the keys to the success of the work ahead. We have to enjoy it.

Chapter 2.10

Beyond Basics- Being Deliberate

Last week I started looking at some of the research information published by Anders Ericsson and Robert Pool in the book, *Peak: Secrets from the New Science of Expertise*. They present three levels of practice: naive, purposeful and deliberate. It is only through that last level that we move beyond just being okay or even good to new levels of "expertise." This goes beyond the supposed "10,000 Hour Rule" that was intuited by Malcolm Gladwell and others from Ericsson's research, as a key to making that level of success. Ericsson points out first that 10,000 hours was an "average" - meaning there were those who had more and those who had less. Beyond that it wasn't just any practice that allowed them to get that far. It was very clear, deliberate and quite intensive practice.

What is deliberate practice then? Well, combining several of Ericsson's and Pool's explanations, here is a summary of the elements of "deliberate" practice.

- Deliberate practice is focused. Students must give it their full attention.
- Deliberate practice involves feedback. Immediate, specific feedback on where students are falling short is vital.
- Deliberate practice requires a teacher
- Deliberate practice requires leaving one's comfort zone. If students aren't pushing themselves beyond what is comfortable and familiar, they will not advance.
- Deliberate practice requires specific goals aimed at target performances
- Deliberate practice builds on mental representations.

I note that in the list there are no suggestions. These are all required. No "electives" on the list. Deliberate practice is not for those just in it for simple fun. It is not for those who want to be casual players. It is for those who want to reach significant levels of expertise in their chosen field. I would say that from my observations over the years in my career fields (ministry and counseling) that these elements hold true for those who end up excelling in those fields. They work at it; they don't take any of it for granted; they are never complacent about what they can do or can accomplish. They will almost always look for new ways to step out of their comfort zones to experience, to learn, to grow, and often to share their expertise. I have no research data to support this- it is what I have seen often. It may be that what many of those have done is just very effective purposeful-type practice, although I would argue that the expanding elements of deliberate practice are also at work- with or without the research data.

Ericsson points out that the research data is rich in certain fields- sports being one; music being another. That is because there are very specific skills and methods of teaching that can be employed in those fields. They can show that taking those extra steps and actions do have real and measurable impacts on the development of expertise.

An important element of why this works is what we now call "brain plasticity." This is the ability of the human brain to grow and change throughout our lifetime. The brain will "rewire" itself with enough practice and exercise. Many of us used to call this "muscle memory" when we would work over and over on a particular passage until it fell just right beneath our fingers. That's part of the brain plasticity. The memory is in the whole interconnection of brain, nerves, and muscles.

Building on basics, one on top of the previous, next on top of what we already know. That's the stretching out of our comfort, the need for feedback, the place of a teacher. But it is also why even the top trumpet players still practice their scales on a daily basis. Many also do a series of routines that keep their skills sharp. Yes, they have played them for years; yes, they do them from memory; no, they are never satisfied that they know them cold. Those basics, whether they are from Arban, Clarke, Schlossberg, or Charlier, are still the basics. These do not change.

What I have discovered, since I am not planning on reaching that very high level of expertise that would require 3-6 hours of practice daily, is that these keep me grounded in my trumpet playing AND in how my abilities are improving. It is these basics that are truly never "just" basic. What Doc or Wynton does is based on those. Everything is built on them. Every time I play those, I need to remember to stay focused. Even the famous Clarke #2. Pay attention. What do I hear differently this time? Why am I having trouble with that particular key today? Why do I forget that particular sharp or flat note? Focus. Give it my full attention. I wish I could say I can do that regularly. I can say I am better today that I was six months ago. If I stay focused, I will continue to improve.

Paying attention is, in and of itself, a source of discomfort- moving out of my easy box. When I pay attention, I don't just go through the exercise and say, "Got it for today. Time to move on." If I am focused, I will notice the tone is off, the breathing isn't falling into place, rhythm skips, or all those missed or sloppy notes. They better get fixed or I will never get it right. That brain plasticity works for the mistakes, too. Mistakes get ingrained if we don't do something to correct them immediately. The single best way to do that is simply to slow down. Still not right? Slower. Remember a few weeks ago when I looked at the three elements of a great trumpet player?

- Great Sound
- Great rhythm
- Great ear.

If tone or sound is off, you need to hear it. If you can't get the rhythm, you need to hear it. If you can't hear it, assume you are playing it too fast. So slow down. In a different context I often quote comedian Lily Tomlin: "For fast relief- try slowing down." It works on trumpet as well as it works in daily life. That is the whole idea of mindfulness, one of those ideas that flow in and out of these posts. More on that again in three weeks. Right now, simply slowing down is the basic. That, in and of itself, can be a stretch for most of us. We want to play at speed, we want to be Dizzy playing a Charlie Parker bebop lick at full speed. Resist that temptation. Learn it first. If the sound and rhythm are off, slow down and get them right. Speed will come- often one beat/minute faster each day.

As I was working on this post, the lead trumpet in the quintet emailed me about having a "trumpet sectional" i.e., the two of us. My first thought was to think back on the quintet's rehearsal the day before. I know that on one of the numbers I was less than good. It is a section and a style that I have trouble with. My response back was "Good idea." It is for the very reasons I have been talking about. I will not get better if I am doing something wrong and not getting feedback- even when I know I haven't done it right. There are the times and places, more than we realize, when we must move to that deliberate practice of getting personal feedback and then working with a colleague on improving it. The email came at the right time. Maybe I should do that more often if I want my practice to be deliberate.

What will be your deliberate practice movement this week? Maybe it will be an extra ten minutes with improving Clarke #2 or working that second section of Charlier at a slow speed in order to get the tone and rhythm, right? Maybe you have a piece coming up in a way-too-soon gig that needs your attention. Don't put it off. Work on it. Be deliberate- and slow- until the brain picks it up. Listen. Hear the good and the not-as-good. Work on fixing it. Get feedback from a colleague or a teacher.

Above all- be deliberate. It's what gets you to your next level.

Next week we will look at more of the elements of deliberate practice and add one more thing: Grit- the thing that keeps us deliberate in our practice.

Chapter 2.11

Staying Mental

Aware that it may be nothing more than beating the same drum over and over, let's take one more look at "deliberate practice." Here again are the standards required of practice to be deliberate:

- Deliberate practice is focused. Students must give it their full attention.
- Deliberate practice involves feedback. Immediate, specific feedback on where students are falling short is vital.
- Deliberate practice requires a teacher
- Deliberate practice requires leaving one's comfort zone. If students aren't pushing themselves beyond what is comfortable and familiar, they will not advance.
- Deliberate practice requires specific goals aimed at target performances
- Deliberate practice builds on mental representations.

One of the most interesting to me is the last one:

Mental representations.

I had never thought of that as part of what practice does. Now I realize that it is something that happens fairly unconsciously. We do build a mental picture of what we are doing. We do look for patterns in the music and, if we are more visually oriented may even construct some mental framework. I noticed myself doing that recently in working on one of our quintet pieces. At one spot in my part, there is a repeating 8th note "D" followed by 3 other 8th notes, then back up to the "D". It repeats this pattern several times. I found myself circling the repeating "D" that gave the section a clear, almost physical structure. It also helped me see that whether notated or not, those "D"s work better with a slight accent so they stand out. After I did it, I realized two things:

1.   It was now easier to play in time and flow because
2.   I now had a mental image in both sound and visual that described the section.

Unless you are already years into being an established and advanced trumpet player, chances are you wouldn't notice that for a while, if ever. All you would have would be the notes on the page. Think now of all those Arban or Clarke exercises that repeat the same pattern across a scale or across the whole set of 12 scales. They build a mental representation. They instill an aural pattern into our subconscious that eventually becomes a natural way of doing the scale. We can all probably play our basic concert Bb scale without even thinking. The fingers just move. But now try to play the concert B scale (our C#/Db). No way can I do that. That physical- and aural- representation isn't there yet. But I keep working at it.

But I am not sure that the best way to keep working at it is by simply reading the notes off the page. This would have sounded like I was thinking crazy not that long ago. I will never be able to remember those scales without having it in front of me. I felt it was absolutely necessary to learn them from the Arban series in exercise 46 on pp. 20-21. It repeats a pattern (visual on the page, aural from the horn) or mental representation, around the circle of 4ths. I got the basics and then closed the book and started working on it by "ear." I still have some difficulty with Db and Gb but it went much faster when I internalized the pattern- a mental representation- and learned it that way. I discovered that also worked well with Clarke #2, the classic exercise that is one of those essentials of trumpet playing. So, it does appear that when we do work toward those mental representations and visualizations, things improve- and often more quickly and effectively than otherwise.

No matter how you do this, though, you are always working on those three "greats":

> Great sound,
> Great rhythm,
> Great listening

Tempo keeps these 3 greats in order. When you get to a difficult place and miss the note, slow it down- it means the tempo was too fast. That also allows those mental representations to catch up to what you are playing. It takes a long time to play as fast as Charlie Parker or Dizzy Gillespie- and do it well. Build the mental representations always, always paying attention to the three greats.

> One more quick thought I heard:
> There is no better motivation for more practice than what happens when you practice more. You won't ever say, "Gee, I wish I hadn't practiced today."

I had said last week that I would talk some about "Grit"- the rest of the *Peak* and deliberate practice story. I think I will hold off on that until sometime in the new year. We've covered a lot of territory on deliberate practice in these three posts. It may be better to work on incorporating these into our own practice time. Grit will then become a refresher and expansion after we get a little more comfortable with being deliberate.

Chapter 2.12

Nothing New- All is New

What has been will be again, what has been done will be done again; there is nothing new under the sun.

-Ecclesiastes 1:9

Many have seen quotes like this one from the preacher in the Biblical book of Ecclesiastes as profoundly depressing. Day by day goes by and there is really nothing new. It's the same old same old day in and day out. But let me suggest that there is another way of looking at it, a way that gets me back to basics and exploring. In the end it will turn into a couple of "new" things:

First, that I can learn from how things were done before. People have been doing what I am doing- how did they grow and learn. That of course is the idea of having mentors, teachers, people to inspire and guide us in what we are doing. It means that there may very well be wisdom in what has gone before. Most of us as trumpet players have been using the Arban's method for years. It was first published around 1859- and is still in print! Charlier, Concone, and others have built on it, but it is still as good as it gets. Nothing new under the sun- just look at Arban.

Second, the preacher of Ecclesiastes can also be saying that if we keep aware of the things around us, we will find something, that for us, is new. Yes, I realize I am reading into the text, not reading from it. But if I know darn well that even if there is nothing new under the sun, I sure haven't learned, seen, or done it all yet. For me, it could be as new as this morning.

But it can be so easy to fall into the trap of thinking that once we have learned something, we can move beyond it- we don't have to keep on working on it. That would be a profound danger for any of us in life- but certainly a potentially musically fatal error as musicians. Reading the stories of people like Miles Davis, John Coltrane, Johann Sebastian Bach seems to show that these great musicians never stopped learning and growing. They were constantly exploring what was already there, it's just that perhaps no one had ever seen it quite that way before. I would describe that to some extent as having a "beginner's mind." There is a Zen Buddhist idea known as "shoshin" - beginner's mind. According to Wikipedia

> it refers to having an attitude of openness, eagerness, and lack of preconceptions when studying a subject, even when studying at an advanced level, just as a beginner in that subject would. (https://en.wikipedia.org/wiki/Shoshin)

Having that beginner's mind is one of those essentials of growing in our trumpet skills. In earlier posts about practicing, I talked about planning as one of the things that sets deliberate (and effective) practice apart from just playing the horn. Let me be clear, I have great difficulty with planning of this sort. I tend to want to move along, not get stuck in "boredom" of practicing too much on one thing. I have been working on this aspect of my musical growth these past 18 months. I am beginning to see the results. (By the way, patience will be one of my topics some week. When I get around to it.) Not just because it has forced me to plan ahead and work on things that are more difficult- an obvious need, but because it has made me look at what is important- and then focus on it. With this in mind, then, I wondered what one of our Shell Lake Trumpet Workshop leaders would add to this. So, I emailed Bill Bergren two questions:

What makes a good plan?

What should be in every trumpet player's plan?

His answer came as no surprise, but rather an important reminder that even when there's nothing new under the sun, there's always the need to be reminded of what is important. He sent me four pillars of what should be in every trumpet player's plan. The first two:

FUNDAMENTALS! 75% The majority of your practice time, 75%, should be spent on fundamentals. If you can play the instrument, you can focus on the musical aspects. This includes routine, scales, method/etude books.

MUSIC! 25% If you are practicing fundamentals in a musical manner, playing actual music should be easy.

Yep. No surprise. Fundamentals, fundamentals, fundamentals. Three things stood out this year in a different way for me when Bill reminded me of these two pillars.

1. These help me play the instrument so that
2. I can learn to play the fundamentals in a musical manner, and
3. This helps me play music musically. Because there is nothing new under the sun, what I will find in some musical piece for band, quintet, etc. will include what I have practiced in the etudes. I remembered one of the pieces the community band played last summer that it felt like a Getchell or Arban's exercise. It made it a lot easier to learn the piece.

I know it sounds strange to think of playing something like an Arban's exercise "musically." We don't think that way when we are looking at the notes and figuring out how to play it. That is why it is important to "read" the piece and then "sing" it first. (Another of Bill Bergren's points from Shell Lake.) Take the time to see and hear the music in the piece so that the music and not just the notes can come out.

It is important to see the etudes we practice as part of the fundamentals. According to Merriam-Webster etude is defined as:

1. a piece of music for the practice of a point of technique
2. a composition built on a technical motive but *played for its artistic value* (Emphasis added)

The word "etude" comes from the French for study. Those etudes from Charlier, Getchell, etc. are meant to be musical so that we can learn techniques-fundamentals. One of my other mentors, Paul Stodolka, also from Shell Lake Trumpet Workshop, commented to me once that when he is finding himself off-center and needing to focus, he goes back to the etudes. It always works.

Bill listed two other pillars that should be part of every trumpet player's plan. These two he said should be separate from the regular practice time:

> LISTENING! ----You need to set aside time every day to listen to good music. It doesn't have to be trumpet players.
> IMPROVISATION! Improvisation is important for ALL players.

A year ago, I would have responded, "Yes, but…" to the second of those pillars. Not because I didn't think it was important, but, well, it just kind of didn't fit into what I was thinking. In reality I was afraid of it! It meant a degree of familiarity with the horn- and music- that I didn't think I could have. Not that I didn't want to learn to improvise, I was just intimidated by it. So, what did. I followed Bill's advice and went back to fundamentals. I learned the 12 major scales. Then I memorized Clarke #2 and one of the exercises doing thirds around the Circle of 4ths. Basic stuff. I worked on trying to play them musically, not just notes being translated from ink to air. It had to move from air to sound to music. I also listened to music. I always do that, but I became far more intentional about what I listened to. I began to concentrate on some specific pieces that had some good- but not complicated- improvisation. That was my plan. It worked.

And what fun it has become.

Next, I'll take a look at what this can mean if we dig even more deeply a allow the beginner's mind to be at work. As always, it will help us be better musicians and be better at living.

Chapter 2.13

Deepening the Beginner's Mind

Before starting last week's post, I did some journaling/scribbling of thoughts. I decided it needed to be a short "poem" in place of the "prose" I generally use. (Poetry is like music in that it forces one to focus on the things that are important without getting into a lot of words- kind of NOT like I am doing here.) Anyway, here's what appeared when I was finished..

Having a beginner's mind-

The mind of a child:

Being childlike,

Filled with wonder- where even the

Old is new

And what's young is filled with wisdom

Do you have any memory of the wonder and awe the first time you heard some music that moved you?

That's beginner's mind.

Do you still have that happen when you hear a performance or recording of someone doing great music?

That's beginner's mind.

Do you still have that happen when you have finished a performance and you sit back in wonder at having been part of the creation of something powerful?

That's beginner's mind.

It happens when the notes fall into place and are no longer just black marks on a white paper. It happens when you wake up one morning and realize that this is a new day of unknown opportunities. It happens when someone points out to you that the trees on that mountain over there are not green- they are an infinite number of colors we call green. That childlikeness is a gift to be nurtured since most of us lose it as we grow older. It doesn't take long for us to get bored with seeing the same things, playing the same songs, looking at the same four walls. Those days we wake up and wonder what's the big deal about another day? We assume it will be just like the ones before. When we do that we lose the childlikeness that EXPECTS each day to be different and can hardly wait to see what it will be.

Do something right there where you are. After reading this paragraph take a look around the room where you are sitting. It is most likely someplace familiar, someplace you may even know like the back of your hand. There's nothing there you haven't seen before. Or is there? Look around- and find one thing that you may never have noticed before- or never saw quite that way until just this moment.

Go ahead. Do it now and then come back. I'll do the same.

How did it go? Find anything? See anything new or unusual or out of place? If not, do it again. Really look hard. There are things there I am sure.

I am sitting at one of my normal coffee shops, one I frequent 3-4 days/week- and have done so for three or more years. Two things showed up in my line-of-sight. First, was a new sign indicating the type of coffee being served this evening. Not unusual, but the sign was new. It didn't have the standard company logo.

The second thing I noticed was an American flag folded in one of those tri-angular display cases made for the flag when it is given to families at a funeral or graveside. What is that doing here, in a coffee shop? Does that framed paper underneath it explain it? I went and looked. It was a flag flown over Operation Resolute Support base in Afghanistan. It was given to a local high school (and this coffee shop) for support of Operation Hometown Gratitude.

That has nothing to do with music. It is the growth of awareness that does. It is sharpening my senses so that I can be more ready to see and hear and experience the life that is around me and within me. How we do anything is how we do everything. Remember that? If the only place and time I try to be mindful is when the trumpet is in my hands, I will probably not be as successful at it as I would like. I will just be playing ink spots on a page or getting whatever sound comes out when I press valves 1 and 3 at the same time. It may sound like music, but it won't be musical. Until I pay attention. Until I know what is inside that note with those valves pressed. Until I know what that sounds like alone- and in a line with other notes. Until I know what those notes sound like when added to other people playing their own notes. Childlikeness. Wonder. Awe.

What surprised me most in that short "poem" above was the way the last two lines flowed out. They came from an awareness- hopefully a mindfulness- of something I hadn't even thought of yet. We are talking about a way of seeing the world around us so that even what is "old is new and what's young is filled with wisdom." This is a mindfulness where we are open to learning from each other and don't put value judgments on what we may see or hear. There is newness even in that same old song I have played a thousand times over the years. How many times has our big band played Glenn Miller's immortal, In the Mood? How many times have all of us played *Stars and Stripes Forever* or the *Star-Spangled Banner*? Do they still move you? Do they still touch that inner place of wonder and awe as if it were the first time you heard them? They can.

Just as the new song or new lick or new flower growing in the spring can be a source of wisdom- learning wise ways that may have never been seen or heard quite that way before. Every March and April I go out looking for signs of spring. I have done this for years and I know what I will find, when it will show up, and where to go to see it. But it is new. New every time. It is a new life. It is a new experience of the world. Returning. Wisdom.

Yes, I am getting philosophical here. Maybe it's the time of the year for that. But when we learn to be mindful and aware in the normal course of each day, each day will no longer be just "normal" but unusual, filled with wonder, and ready to move us into new understandings of who we are. Tomorrow, when I pick up Clarke #2 there will be something there to change my perception. It will even be there in the long tones I start with. As I cultivate that in all I do each day, I will grow- and so will my music.

Chapter 2.14

From the Audience

We all know that listening to good music performances is an important part of being a good musician. It isn't just about what *we* play- it is about learning the many nuances of musical language. It is also about experiencing the many languages of different musical genres. I feel sad for people who can't or don't enjoy many types of music. They are missing out on so many different ways of experiencing the wonders of music.

This past week was a week of music to listen to. We were visiting friends in Pennsylvania and had the opportunity to attend three musical events with them- two Christmas Vesper services and one orchestral concert. The one vesper was one I myself had participated in over 40 years ago as a scripture reader. It is for me the paradigm of a Christmas Eve-type vespers service in my own faith tradition. The congregational hymns resonate deeply in my own spiritual life. But more than that the whole vespers expresses a deep connection with tradition.

That was also true in the second Christmas vesper service at another nearby university. They have the same long-standing tradition of particular songs and musical accompaniment. I had never been to that particular vespers before.

But it, too, resonated deeply- being performed in a wonderful imitation Gothic structure built in the late 1800s. Like all such religious buildings they can be called, as this church once was, a "sermon in stone."

These vespers services underscore the importance of tradition in music. Even when we are writing new compositions or improvising a jazz solo, we are part of a tradition. We stand in an incredible line of musicians and music lovers. We are not alone- and don't need to be alone. We are part of something far greater than ourselves which moves us.

The orchestral event was truly an event. It was the Lehigh University Philharmonic doing Mahler's 6th! It was in the performance hall with 100+ musicians on stage and a sound that is as good as any. When doing Mahler, one needs to be in shape. When one listens to Mahler, one must also be in shape. (The Mahler was the middle day of the three events, bookended on Friday and Sunday by the two vespers services.) For a musician being in the audience was nothing short of heavenly. The opportunity to hear so many different styles of instrumental, orchestral, and choral music in such a short time is priceless. Placing them in historic places or fine examples of musical venues makes it even more so.

Before talking about what I learned, I need to make one idea very clear. To me, listening to music is NOT a passive experience. Music is never a spectator sport. I move to the beat, I direct the sounds, I allow my eyes to close and just let the sounds envelope me. It is impossible for me to be passive. (My wife often insists on holding my hand during a concert to at least keep me in some sense of control. It doesn't often work well.) Music is not meant to be something that is just there. It is the world and the word turned into movement; it is the frequency of life vibrating. How can I not move with it?

What then did I learn from this marathon music weekend? To be honest, nothing unique. Instead, what I learned was a reinforcement of much of what this whole Tuning Slide blog has been about for the last year and a half. There are things that we musicians need to remember when attending a concert or musical event. They are very simple, but profound in their depth. As you sit in such an event:

- Let the music flow.

Don't try to control what you are hearing. Don't work on figuring out the "wow!" moments. Just let them happen as they will. If it helps to close your eyes from time to time to feel the flow, do it. But pay attention to where and how it is flowing. No, I can't explain it any better than that. Pay attention to the dynamics and the way one part flows into the next. Any well-planned and -performed concert will flow. Music will, too.

- Watch the musicians

There were a couple very powerful musicians in the philharmonic that lived the music as they were playing it. They wanted to make sure the music moved the way they wanted us to hear it. You could see it on their faces; the way the one played the oboe was almost magical; the principal trumpet and horn players were coaxing every ounce of themselves out of their horns; the lead violinist put his whole body into every important moment. The singers were harder to discern in the darkened churches, but the smiles and wonder in their voices was spectacular even when I couldn't see them.

- Listen to the emotions

Putting the flow in with the musicians you get emotion. The emotion the musicians are playing with- and the emotion in the original music. Both vespers services ended with what, for them, are traditional pieces. Yet they sounded like they were being sung for the first time. The musicians in the Mahler, guided by a very skilled conductor, phrased every up and down of emotion. It was a joy in all these instances to allow those emotions to well up within me.

- Expect the soul to be moved

Don't ever go into a concert expecting nothing to happen. Expect to be moved; be open to it. Sure, it doesn't always work that way, but the chances are a great deal better that it will of you go in with your soul or spirit primed to be moved.

These are for us as audience members. But we are also musicians ourselves. As a musician, this week reminded me of the order of things that we heard about at the Trumpet Workshop.

1. The music is first
2. The other musicians are second.
3. The audience is third
4. You are fourth.

Combing these with the four things I mentioned to be prepared for when you attend a concert, here is what it means when you are the musician performing for that audience out there.

- **As a musician always respect the music. It's not about you!** The music, in and of itself has power and demands respect. It can be Mahler, an old plainsong, a hymn written in the 1700s, or a prelude composed specifically for this event. Respect it. It has its own life and power. Don't get in the way.
- **Be humble. It's not about you!** Yes, I know. Trumpet players are not known for their humility. All the more reason to remember this. The music is not about any one of us individually. You and I are part of an ensemble. We play together to evoke the emotions that are already there in the music. We are there to tap into the power of those notes working together and then share it. If I get so excited or overwhelmed by my own part or my own greatness, it all gets lost.
- **Study the parts. Learn them as if they are friends.** Commit yourself to them. One of the students in the philharmonic was asked how much time they devoted to learning the Mahler. He said they practiced 3 1/2 hours per week for 3 1/2 months. That is over 50 hours of rehearsal time- not including the time the musicians worked on it by themselves. That is when and how a piece comes together. It is not magic or rocket

science or even just having a bunch of really talented musicians. It's hard work for hour upon hour, week upon week. In so doing they learned what Mahler may have been trying to communicate. Then they shared it with us.

- **Stay focused. Be aware that you are a conduit for the spirit of the music to reach others.** They are depending on you to do that. That's why the audience is there. It is for them. It is your opportunity to give them your best- individually and as a group. It is your sharing the wonder of the music- paying it forward.

Think on these things at your next performance. Large or small, it will make it a better experience for you and your audience. Enjoy your music as much as you enjoy music played by others.

If you are interested, here are links to previous performances of the two vesper services on YouTube.

Moravian College (2014) (https://youtu.be/-0as51lBRPM)

Lehigh University closing (2015) (https://youtu.be/YdsR1jGSbFk)

Chapter 2.15

Give Yourself a Gift

Stephen Covey, educator and speaker, wrote one of the basic books on self-management in 1989, *The 7 Habits of Highly Effective People*. This week I simply want to think about the 7th habit which he called "Sharpening the Saw"-continually improving what we do and who we are.

On the Change Management Coach website, counseling psychologist and life coach Mark Connelly described it this way: (http://www.change-management-coach.com/stephen-covey.html)

> Habit 7 is about looking after yourself. You are the greatest asset you have and we have to learn to take time to look after ourselves. Stephen Covey suggests we pay attention to four areas in our lives:
>
> **Physical:** *Exercise, Nutrition, Stress Management*
>
> **Spiritual:** *Value Clarification and Commitment, Study and Meditation*
>
> **Mental:** *Reading, Visualizing, Planning, Writing*
>
> **Social/Emotional:** *Service, Empathy, Synergy, Intrinsic Security.*

Not a bad idea to consider this season. I have noticed that for many people this year's season has been more low-key than usual. Several have said to me that the intensity and downright unusual behavior of the recent election campaign have worn us down. Energy levels have been depleted. The stress and tension evident in so many places can fog our brains and actions. We may find ourselves sitting and just wondering about everything and nothing. The physical, spiritual, mental, and social/emotional assets have been nearly exhausted. Many look around and wonder what happened to them and to the world we used to know. It feels dark- or at least gray and uncertain.

Yet this is a season of light. The three major holidays in the next two weeks are celebrations of light coming into the darkness. The Christmas season vibrates with light from stars, candles, and the hint of angels' trumpets. The Jewish celebration of Hanukkah is called the Feast of Lights, celebrating the miracle of light in a dark time. The African-American Kwanzaa, celebrating its 50th year this year, lights seven candles, bringing the light of the principles of the holiday season.

In addition to light and celebration of hope and unity and peace, gift-giving is very much a part of all three holidays. So, let me suggest that Covey's 7th habit could also be described as giving yourself a gift and sharing your gift of yourself with others. As musicians we can be overly busy this season- but perhaps it can be seen as bringing the light of music to others. That shift in perspective can go a long way to changing how we see what we are doing. For example, I have been looking forward to playing with our quintet in church on Christmas morning. It is a gift to myself to be able to play the seasonal music in public. It is a gift to my own spiritual life to do it in church- even a church that is not part of my own tradition. It is a gift I am excited to share with those in church that morning. It is not a burden- it is a gift-receiving and gift-giving joy.

Then there are the many other ways we can gift ourselves this season. We can find those moments of rest and relaxation. Maybe we will have time to do some exercise or getting outdoors. (The physical.) We can look around and give thanks for what we have been given. We can celebrate our own spiritual and communal traditions and renew our commitments to our family, friends, and communities. (The spiritual.) We might want to take time to do some reading or meditating or listening to some good music. (The mental.) We can find ways to reach out to others, either with our music, a phone call, or connecting with friends. (The social.)

We need to take care of ourselves. That is not an end in itself. It is part of who we are. We need to be healthy for ourselves and to be able to share with others. We are social beings. We are spiritual beings. We are physical beings. All these come together when we keep ourselves as healthy and focused as we can.

Take care of yourselves. It has been a tough few month. Be good to yourself and those around you. You will be richly blessed.

Christmas. Hanukkah. Kwanzaa.

Celebrate the light and hope and peace within and around you.

Oh- and make sure you play your trumpet. That may be the most important gift to give yourself this year.

Chapter 2.16

Looking Both Ways

Steve Jobs famously once said:

> You can only connect the dots looking backward. Just make good dots.

My thought when I heard that was that in order to be successful you need to look both ways, just like we were always told when crossing the street. Here, though the looking is back and ahead. Looking back connects the dots, as Jobs indicated, helping us to see what we did (or didn't do) to get where we are today. Looking ahead helps us think about where we want to be in the future. Many of us do that at certain times of the year- birthdays, anniversaries. But most of us do it this week between Christmas and New Year. Another year has passed, the year ahead is a so-called "blank slate".

The subject reminded me of a saying I heard at Shell Lake last summer:

> Whenever you go through a door- you will see four more doors appear.

There is a sense in that which says that we are never finished- when we make progress, we can see the progress we need to make. When we make progress, when we are successful or improve at what we are doing, we can see the new possibilities that lie ahead of us. And those possibilities multiply as we go through each door of progress.

Last year, for example, I made it my goal to learn the twelve major scales. I made it very successfully through that door. After that initial success I decided that advance in my skill led me to at least two more opportunities. One was to memorize Clarke #2- a great way to add to my skills at the scales. The other was that I found myself able to improvise on different scales more easily. Each of those doors has now led me to new confidence.

But there was a door I didn't go through quite as well as I had hoped. I wrote earlier in the year about my "performance anxiety" and that over the years it doesn't matter how well I know a piece, the move from the practice room to the performance venue never goes as well as I would like it to. I never play in performance as well as (I think) I do in practice. It happened again on Christmas and I found myself starting to slide back into the old thinking. "I'll never get past it. I'm not as good as I think I am." But looking back, I managed to say, "Not true!" Looking back and connecting the dots, I saw the Vintage Band Festival in July when I did the solo part of the Canadian Brass version of "Amazing Grace." No accompaniment, no rhythm, just me starting out and playing. I can do it. I have made it through that door far better than I am willing to accept when I have a glitch. So, what's wrong? What is the next door ahead of me that this has brought me to?

See how it works? Connecting the dots as we look back helps us discover what we need to be doing ahead of us.

Take time this week then to first ask yourself:

- What doors did you go through this past year?
- How far have you come?
- What's new about you this year?
- What doors are now opened that you couldn't have walked through last year at this time?
- So what?

Looking at progress helps you see what you are still capable of doing.

Looking at when we didn't do as much as we wanted gets us looking at what we can do to change that. There's an old saying:

Doing what you've always done will only get you what you have always gotten.

At that point we often rationalize or make an excuse why we aren't doing something- "I can't do that!"

In my examples of movement this year I have decided the next stage of work will be to learn the minor and 7th chords across the 12 keys. I'm still exploring the ways of doing that, but I know it is at the top of the goals for 2017. I have also been working on learning a solo from a recording I admire and enjoy. That is the next of my goals for the beginning of the new year- finish learning that and then adapting it for myself. And third, the performance issue. I realized that most of the time now it has nothing to do with how I'm feeling about myself or my ability; it is about how I focus- or don't- getting ready for a performance. My third goal is only partially related to my music- it's about focus and building my inner ability to do so. I have a couple things I want to do in that area and learn how to apply it to my performance.

Goals. That's the other half of looking both ways. They are today's dots leading to the ones we haven't put down yet. That is how we make good dots that connect us from where we have been to what can yet become.

May you all have a Happy New Year- making music, enjoying music, and turning them all into the excitement and hope for you.

Chapter 2.17

Falling Forward

Google "goal-setting". There can be:

- Seven types of goals;
- Four types of goals;
- lifetime, long-term and short-term goals;
- outcome, process, or performance goals....

On and on it can go. Goals need to be

- Specific and achievable;
- Measurable and realistic...
- etc., etc., etc.....

As we start a new year, we often hear about all those great new year's res-olutions- that are only too soon forgotten. Anyone who has been a regular at a gym will tell you the worst time of the year is January when all those people who have decided to get healthy show up. Give them a month or so and things will quiet down.

Resolutions, though, aren't goals. Resolutions are ways of wishing and hoping. That's why they usually fail. And when they fail, we give up on them. Guess I'm not going to do THAT this year. We move on.

Perhaps that is one of the greatest differences between resolutions and goals. When we set a goal, we are also setting in place the possibility of failure- and if we are honest- we know that. But when we set goals, the failures are planned for.

Several of the faculty talked about some of this at last year's Shell Lake workshop. I went back to my notebook from the week and came across this series of notes and reflections on the important place "failures" have in helping us reach our goals:

- **Goals take time.** They have failure moments along the way. Success is moving through the failures and using them for your benefit. The famous remark from Thomas Edison that he didn't have failures, he just knew many things that don't work.

- **How did your failures help shape you?** I was set on being an engineer when I graduated from high school in 1966. Everyone who had any kind of chance to go to college in those years was directed toward engineering or science. The space race spurred it; American pride accelerated it. After two years it was more than clear that I was not cut out to be an engineer. It wasn't how I thought. Some of my family saw that as failure. I was not going to make it in the world with a degree in political science. I was a disappointment.

- **Figure out a different way.** Which is what I eventually did. I didn't give up on life or whatever. Over the next four years I finished college and found something that did fit the way I work and think. I entered seminary and went on to a very satisfying, challenging, and exciting career.

- **Change your perspective.** Management guru John Maxwell wrote a whole book about this- Failing Forward: Turning Mistakes Into Stepping Stones for Success. Failure is in giving up, not getting back up. Success- at its very basic is continuing to put one foot in front of the other, even when it doesn't look like it's going the right direction.

- **There are valleys between mountaintops.** That is one of the more subtly profound statements I wrote in my notebook. The metaphorical mountaintops lead to valleys. The valleys are the places where we can learn to take the next step toward what we saw from the mountaintop.
- **To realize you suck at something- you're on the right track.** It was when I heard a recording of our quintet and the poor quality of my sound that I realized I needed to do something. I didn't hear that when I was playing live. The same thing happened when I heard my solo on Basin Street Blues with the big band for the first time. In my ear- it sucked! I didn't like it. It had no life. It sounded tired. If I had never heard that and realized how poor it sounded, I might never have started on this journey that has now gone through two summers of Shell Lake camps and incredible hours of practice in ways I never have done before.

That's the simple process of failure and success. I was in my mid-60s when that all began. It could have been discouraging. I could have said "The hell with it!" But I had a greater goal, one of those big ones- to truly be a musician in ways unlike any time in my life. It can be called perseverance, or grit, or stubborn, ideas I will deal with later this winter and spring. It is just following the goals and dreams into something new and different.

Have goals and act on them. Prioritize, them, of course. I have never been able to memorize. That doesn't mean I can't. At this point in my musical life, there are other things more important than taking the time needed to learn how to do that. My goals are in scales and arpeggios, improvising and endurance, fun and performance. I keep thinking about memorization, but it's not a priority. Yet.

As we start 2017 in our musical journeys:

- We start something by taking the necessary steps to get there.
- We have to know where we want to go.
- We then create opportunities then things happen.
- We follow our interests and take risks.

Happy New Year! Let's continue to make music- and life.

Chapter 2.18

As Simple As...

It is one of Mr. Baca's favorite insights at Shell Lake Trumpet Workshop:

> Make everything sound like Mary Had A Little Lamb. A 3-year-old
> can sing it without thinking about it. Put the rhythm on the board for a
> new player and they will struggle with it.

And we all know it's true.

All those black marks on the page are intimidating.

All those sharps or flats? No way!

Look at the tempo marking. Are they kidding?

How am I ever going to get that down in time for the concert?

Excuses, excuses, excuses. But they work. We don't ever learn it like we could. We don't take the time to practice like we need to. We continue to assume that it is too hard because we think it's too hard and therefore it remains too hard.

No, this is not another post on practicing. That's still a few weeks away. It is another post reminding us to keep ourselves in the right balance with the right kind of goals. It is a reminder that just practicing any old thing will just get us any old someplace- or nowhere near where we want to be.

Last week in looking at planning for the new year I wrote:

> We start something by taking the necessary steps to get there.
> We have to know where we want to go.
> We then create opportunities then things happen.
> We follow our interests and take risks.

One of those places we want to go is to make everything as natural as Mary Had a Little Lamb (or Twinkle, Twinkle.) No matter what the piece is that we are working on, it is the feel of the natural that we want. I used to joke when I heard a trumpet player do something extraordinary that "those notes aren't in my trumpet." I was trying to be funny. But I was also trying to make a feeble excuse for myself. If they aren't in my trumpet then I don't have to work on them or learn to play them. Simple? Yes. But also self-defeating. It's almost like saying,

> "My goal is to be as mediocre as I feel I am. I want to continue to suck at being a trumpet player."

A website, Cyber PR (http://cyberprmusic.com/musicians-guide-setting-achieving-goals-2016/) posted last year on ideas for setting musical goals. They suggested a few steps:

Find your focus areas (You are creating a sense of order)

Write the goals down. (Journals, paper or virtual, are a great idea.)

Start with an easy goal and do it on a timeline

Keep moving by keeping lists for each goal

Look at the goals daily

Look for people to help you achieve the goals- your "team"

Plan for the time to do what you want

So, after finding that I came up with my focus list for musicians to consider. I wrote them in the first person since they are my way of finding some focus.

Listen to the kind of music I want to know or play better, which is (or should be) basically all music

Take time to sing

Find my weak spots

Develop a plan to improve the weak spots.

Try some memory work

Write some licks, choruses or songs

Here's one thing that came out of that:

I was listening to a folk version of the song the Beach Boys interpreted in Sloop John B. I noticed that it had a different feel from the Beach Boys' version. I also noticed that I liked the way the arrangement fell into place with the different voices. [This is the first item above. I love to listen to music, but as a musician I am also trying to listen differently than I used to. Hence, I noticed things about the song that intrigued me. Yes, I sang along!]

It might be fun to learn the song on my trumpet. [This helps me address a couple of my growth areas- playing by ear, memorizing a song, expanding my musical vocabulary.]

I then thought that it also might be a fun piece to work into a number for the brass quintet, maybe even trying to put different sections into different styles allowing the different voices of the different instruments to stand out individually. [I now move into the area of taking what I hear and discover into writing it down- and adding other parts that also require a closer listening and more learning by ear. It will also help me understand a little more music theory, chord, melody structure, etc. An important area for my own growth!]

I have a couple months coming up when I will have more time than usual to do the learning and writing. [A timeline- by the end of March to have a first draft ready for the quintet to play.]

Hence, I have come up with a goal and a plan to address some of my own joys and areas for evolution.

Right now, that all looks and feels a lot like a full score of Les Mis printed on one page. But with my goals set down for you (and me) to see, I have a plan to turn it into Mary Had a Little Lamb. It of course is one of several goals in my focus for the next couple months, but this is a new and challenging area for me. I expect it will also have impacts on my other areas of advancement.

To learn to do this in music is a great way of learning to do it in other areas. I have already learned ways of doing this kind of planning and focus in my career and personal life. I bring it to my musical life, improve the process, and take it on to other things as well. This is the cross-fertilization that naturally occurs in our daily living. We are internally interconnected. Allow each to nourish the others. You will keep your life in tune.

What is your plan for the next three months? Where do you need to focus? Who can help you develop it? What's keeping you from doing it?

Go and do it!

Chapter 2.19

Playing Together

- Steve Carlton was one of the premier pitchers of the 1960s to 1980s. In 1972, with the Philadelphia Phillies Carlton had a win-loss record of 27-10 and a remarkable earned run average of 1.97. When Carlton did not pitch the team was 32-87. No pitcher in the twentieth century has won as high a proportion of his team's victories (45.8%).
- In 2016 Brian Dozier had 42 home runs, the best of his career. He was tied for 3rd in major league baseball. His team, the Minnesota Twins floundered at the bottom of the league.

As great and wonderful as these statistics are for the individual player, they show something else. It is very difficult for a team to make it if they only have one great player. Carlton, Dozier, and others like them stand out because they have a great deal of talent that can surpass the teams they play with. But the team needs more than they are capable of giving.

I thought of this again as I looked at those four things we as musicians are supposed to pay attention to:

> Music was #1
> Fellow musicians #2
> The audience is #3 and
> You, the individual musician, are #4.

In other words, it isn't all about me. It is "us."

Jason Bergman, in the October 2016 Journal of the International Trumpet Guild, interviewed the trumpet section of the Dallas Symphony. Ryan Anthony, principal trumpet said,

> You know, a principal player is only as good as the section. Specifically, he's as good as the second trumpet allows him to be. It's always up to Kevin how well I'm going to do. I always trust Kevin and know that any time I sound good it's because he's right there with me. (ITG Journal, October, 2016, p. 90)

Music is #1, but who you are playing alongside is #2. In order to perform the best that you can, and do justice to the music itself, you have to be aware of what the other musicians are doing. You have to know your place in the piece and your role in the group. I said earlier this season that a composer writes a fourth part for a reason- she wants a fourth part; it does something for the music. Whatever part you are playing can seriously impact the other musicians, the music, what the audience hears, and finally your own feelings about what you are doing. See how all four of those fit together?

It happened to me again on Christmas. The quintet was playing a really fun and exciting piece as our final prelude number. Somewhere, somehow about 8 measures into the piece I had a very brief moment when I defocused. My ADD had a "squirrel" moment. In a piece like that, even a brief mini-second is enough to get lost. I got lost. Because it was a newer number I was not as clued into the whole sound of the group as I could be. It was not a big disaster, but it was enough. For about 16 or so measures the group was relatively lost. The congregation listening to us might have just thought that it was a kind of weird arrangement. As a group, though, we had some difficulty getting back together until what was obviously a transition point in the piece.

It ended well. The brass accompaniment to the opening and closing hymns was superb. No one but us will probably ever remember the prelude falling apart. But I re-learned several things in the process:

1. Focus is essential. Maintaining it can be tough. I have come to realize that a significant part of what used to be "performance anxiety" has become more like the inability to stay focused. I can get distracted by a movement in the audience. I don't usually get distracted by my own thoughts, although it does happen. When I think of it as "performance anxiety" then I do get distracted by myself. But it is usually that other movement. It is one of the things I must work on. I am better, but I am still working on it.

2. Rehearsal is essential. As we have heard, practice is for us to learn our part; rehearsal is to learn how our part fits with everyone else's. Obviously, I have gotten lost before in a performance. (See #1). In a number of our pieces, we all know the piece well enough to get back without a train wreck. For me, this incident showed how important those rehearsals are for the sound of the whole group together! If I know my part well enough, I can then stay focused at rehearsal and know the rest of the parts.

3. Don't panic. I have learned not to react when I get defocused. When I was younger, I tended to feel like the world had just fallen apart and was only going to get worse. It is impossible to regain any focus when that happens. The fight or flight syndrome will automatically kick in. Mindfulness, stress reduction, centering can then be used to stop the panic. With enough practice of doing this when panic isn't happening, just a quick breath, switch in thought, or some internal cue can bring things back to center.

4. Listen. When I am no longer on the edge of some form of panic, self-induced or other, I can take a moment and hear what's happening. If my time in rehearsal has been effective, I can more easily find my way back to where I'm supposed to be. The feel of the piece, the forward movement of the song, the groove at work will guide me in the right direction.

5. Get focused again. With all things back in place- or heading in that direction, it's back to focus and move on. The music regains its #1 place, I am in tune with the other musicians (#2), the audience gets to hear the music (#3), and I'm in the right place in my head. (#4)

It takes longer to write or read this than it does for it to happen. Like all else in what we are doing, we need to develop the skills. Next week I will look at some of the ways we can learn and develop those skills. That is important since performance is not the only place where we can get defocused, lost in our thoughts, issues, problems, or stress. How we do anything can become how we do everything!

Chapter 2.20

Growing Mindfulness

As you begin to realize that every different type of music, everybody's individual music, has its own rhythm, life, language and heritage, you realize how life changes, and you learn how to be more open and adaptive to what is around us.

-Yo-Yo Ma

Becoming open and adaptive the what is around us is a goal for every musician. A good word for it is mindfulness. In the ongoing spirit of this blog where tuning ourselves helps us be in tune with our music- and vice versa, I am going to step away from music for most of this post and talk about being mindful. Don't forget- how you do anything is how you do everything. Therefore, if you do anything with mindfulness, you will learn to do everything with mindfulness. The result will be that you are a better musician and a better person.

Let's start with a reminder of what mindfulness is. The person who has introduced mindfulness to millions is Jon Kabat-Zinn. His classic definition is simple and to the point.

Mindfulness is awareness that arises through

- Paying attention,
- On purpose,
- In the present moment,
- Non-judgmentally. It's about knowing what is on your mind.

How can we learn this? I found a web site called Zen Habits (https://zen-habits.net/ritual/) that lists some possible "rituals" that can help develop mindfulness. Here are a few of them that can be important for our developing musician mindfulness.

It's good to start the day being mindful. Zen Habits suggests two mindful actions. (Original comments in italics; mine within brackets.):

> *Sit in the morning. When you wake up, in the quiet of the morning, perhaps as your coffee is brewing, get a small cushion and sit on the floor. I will often use this opportunity to stretch, as I am very inflexible. I feel every muscle in my body, and it is like I am slowly awakening to the day. I'll also just sit, and focus on my breathing going in and out. [I'll have more on mindfulness meditation again on a future post.]*
>
> *Brush your teeth. I assume we all brush our teeth, but often we do it while thinking of other things. Try fully concentrating on the action of brushing, on each stroke of each tooth, going from one side of the mouth to the other. You end up doing a better job, and it helps you realize how much we do on autopilot. [Here is a good example of how we do anything can impact everything. Just being mindful of brushing can train us to focus the mind.]*

As you go through your day, take time for these:

> *Walk slowly. I like to take breaks from work, and go outside for a little walk. Walk slowly, each step a practice in awareness. Pay attention to your breathing, to everything around you, to the sounds and light and texture of objects.* [Slow walking is great for feeling the body in motion. It can help us begin to "feel" what our body "feels" like. That is an important part of playing music- knowing what how our body is feeling and responding.]

> *Read in silence. Find a quiet time (mornings or evenings are great for me), and a quiet spot, and read a good novel. Have no television or computers on nearby, and just immerse yourself in the world of the novel. It might seem contradictory to let your mind move from the present into the time of the novel, but it's a great practice in focus.* [Just an "Amen!" to that! Note, though, that this isn't studying or reading to learn- it is for enjoyment.]

As you think about your day, Zen Habits suggests practicing your ability to focus. This one might be helpful if you have a significant concert or performance coming and you need to get the feel of it.

> *Work with focus. Start your workday by choosing one task that will make a big difference in your work, and clearing everything else away. Just do that one task, and don't switch to other tasks.* [Then apply this to your music practice. Simple, yes, but it takes practice.]

Dr. Amit Sood, one of my mentors from Mayo Clinic, suggests that we should have a specific "theme" for each day of the week and stay focused on that through the day. His weekly list is

> *Monday: Gratitude*
> *Tuesday: Compassion*
> *Wednesday: Acceptance*
> *Thursday: Higher Meaning*
> *Friday: Forgiveness*
> *Saturday: Celebration*
> *Sunday: Reflection*

If you start each day aware of the theme and learn to work on that for the day, in a few weeks all of the themes will be woven into the fabric of each day. It's just like highlighting one part for each day. Then, with another few weeks practice you will know which of these is needed on any given day or even part of the day.

The goal of all this is that non-judgmental awareness- mindfulness. As you develop these skills, they will have a positive impact on your musicianship. Your musicality will be more even and not as dependent on "getting in the right mood" since you will have more awareness of how to focus on what is in front of you. It won't be pulled down by other people as acceptance and compassion will be there. You will find yourself more balanced as you discover the greater meaning in your day and your music, celebrating what you are given the chance to do. Reflection on your life and music will help you be more forgiving of others- and most importantly of yourself.

There is a comfort, peace and joy in deepening the ability to mindful. It gives each moment the possibility of new discoveries. It keeps us focused on what is in front of us, and it allows us to build today what will be good for us tomorrow. No judgement. Just start with what is and move from there.

Chapter 2.21

You Gotta Have Grit

"Grit is about working on something you care about so much that you're will-ing to stay loyal to it."

"It's doing what you love. I get that."

"Right, it's doing what you love, but not just falling in love—staying in love." (Grit, p. 53)

Back in November I did some posts on "deliberate practice" as being one of the most significant keys to developing skills. It isn't 10,000 hours, it how you spend those 10,000 hours. That was taken from the book, *Peak: Secrets from the New Science of Expertise* by Anders Ericsson and Robert Pool. They clearly believe- and can show- that there is not such a thing as "natural talent. It takes work- and lots of it.

Another book from last year takes this to a different level. Angela Duck-worth, in her book, *Grit: The Power of Passion and Perseverance* asks the excellent next question. "How do you stay motivated to practice all those hours?" Ericsson and Pool raised the same issue when they noted that this "deliberate practice" is not always fun or easy. You have to keep working at it. Duckworth digs deeply into what she calls "grit."

Like Ericsson and Pool, she demythologizes "natural talent.

> Nietzsche said. "For if we think of genius as something magical, we are not obliged to compare ourselves and find ourselves lacking. . ... To call someone 'divine' means: 'here there is no need to compete.'"
>
> In other words, mythologizing natural talent lets us all off the hook."
>
> (Grit, pp. 43-44)

Great quote, and right on target. I can never be as good as [fill in the blank] because they have natural talent. Even trumpet players, known for our supposedly over-sized egos, may try to imitate Doc, Miles, or Maynard, "but you know- those guys had natural talent. I can never do what they do."

Malarkey Nietzsche says. As do Ericsson and Duckworth and many others. There may be other reasons why we may not end up at the level of the greats, but natural talent isn't one of them.

After showing her reasons why she doesn't accept "natural talent, Duckworth went on to study "grit", stick-to-itiveness, motivation in many different areas. When she got to music, she affirmed Ericsson's ideas. She then lists four barriers, "buzz-killers" she calls them, that keep us from sticking to the long haul.

> "I'm bored."
>
> "The effort isn't worth it."
>
> "This isn't important to me."
>
> "I can't do this, so I might as well give up." (Grit, p. 80)

I don't know about you, but any one of those can- and does- crop up on a much too regular basis. These are the questions raised by the inner voice that tells us we aren't good enough or that fears failing. In the book *The Inner Game of Music*, Barry Green calls this voice Self 1. It is the voice of interference. On the

251

other hand, there is Self 2, the voice of our talents, abilities, desires, grace. The trick is giving Self 2 the go-ahead and bringing Self 1 along. Duckworth then writes (with my comments in between):

> ...the research reveals the psychological assets that mature paragons of grit have in common. There are four. They counter each of the buzz-killers listed above, and they tend to develop, over the years, in a particular order.
>
> **First comes interest.** Passion begins with intrinsically enjoying what you do. Every gritty person I've studied can point to aspects of their work they enjoy less than others, and most have to put up with at least one or two chores they don't enjoy at all. Nevertheless, they're captivated by the endeavor as a whole. With enduring fascination and childlike curiosity, they practically shout out, "I love what I do!"

I love the phrase "enduring fascination and childlike curiosity." Remember last week and the discussion on mindfulness? This fascination and curiosity is part of what we are building when we practice mindfulness. (By the way, how are you doing at developing that? Just thought I'd ask.) Not everything we do is exciting and adrenaline producing (think- long tones.) There are aspects of every job that are mundane and, yes, boring. But there is that initial interest. Don't lose it. Stay mindful

> **Next comes the capacity to practice.** One form of perseverance is the daily discipline of trying to do things better than we did yesterday. So, after you've discovered and developed interest in a particular area, you must devote yourself to the sort of focused, full-hearted, challenge-exceeding-skill practice that leads to mastery. You must zero in on your weaknesses, and you must do so over and over again, for hours a day, week after month after year. To be gritty is to resist complacency. ""Whatever it takes, I want to improve!" is a refrain of all paragons of grit, no matter their particular interest, and no matter how excellent they already are.

For some of us the capacity to practice may be greater than for others. If you have a 40-hour a week job, you won't be able to put in four hours of practice every day. But there has to be a discipline of doing it- and seeking to do it better than the day before. This goes on month after month. There are days when we don't want to pick up that horn and go through the routine. But I have never met anyone who was sorry they did when they finished.

> **Third is purpose.** What ripens passion is the conviction that your work matters. For most people, interest without purpose is nearly impossible to sustain for a lifetime. It is therefore imperative that you identify your work as both personally interesting and, at the same time, integrally connected to the well-being of others. For a few, a sense of purpose dawns early, but for many, the motivation to serve others heightens after the development of interest and years of disciplined practice. Regardless, fully mature exemplars of grit invariably tell me, "My work is important—both to me and to others."

Why am I doing this? I am sixty-eight years old. I will never be at the level of my trumpet heroes. Why is it important for me to get out that horn and practice every day? If I was just doing it for my ego reward of sitting in my practice room and hitting a high C on a regular basis, I would soon lose interest. Even (finally) being able to play Al Hirt's *Java* never kept me going. But ever since I have been playing in groups- concert bands, big bands, a quintet- I have begun to (re)discover the joy of playing for others, of watching an audience respond, and yes, the ego reward of playing more challenging music. I may never play the Charlier etude in public, but it gives me the skill to play Copland or Gabrieli.

> *And, finally, hope.* Hope is a rising-to-the-occasion kind of perseverance. In this book, I discuss it after interest, practice, and purpose—but hope does not define the last stage of grit. It defines every stage. From the very beginning to the very end, it is inestimably important to learn to keep going even when things are difficult, even when we have doubts. "At various points, in big ways and small, we get knocked down. If we stay down, grit loses. If we get up, grit prevails." (Grit, pp. 80-82)

Again, a great phrase- hope "defines every stage" of grit. Yes, I have blown solos with the band, or missed entrances with the quintet. Yes, some days my embouchure just doesn't want to cooperate. Does any of that mean I have reached the end of my skill development? I HOPE not. When I have gone as far as I think I am able to go, grit will lose. I have always wanted to be a skilled musician. Other passions, such as my career vocation, were more important. Now, with time and practice, I have the hope that this dream will continue to be fulfilled.

Could I have done this earlier? Sure, but I wasn't ready, I guess. The old saying- when the student is ready the teacher(s) will appear- is true. I didn't know it was possible. Now I do. I have lived this way in my vocations. Those four things of interest, practice, purpose, and hope led me through over 40 years in my careers of choice. No matter what you or I do for a living, we can apply them there- and in whatever else may be important to us.

Just don't quit.

Chapter 2.22

Beginning With Air

I had a request a couple weeks ago for an idea for the Tuning Slide. It came from one of the students at last year's Trumpet Workshop at Shell Lake, WI. Not one to ignore one of my one or two fans, I thought I would give it a go.

One of the days at camp Bill Bergren taught one of the permanent Shell Lake staff how to play a trumpet. The staff member had never played trumpet before. He was a musician, played bass as I remember it. But had never played a wind instrument. Bill is an excellent teacher in the Bill Adam tradition and is a former student of Mr. Adam. It was quite a "demonstration." Perhaps some of the high school and college-age students can remember their first struggles with the trumpet. I cannot. It is a dim and clouded place in history, fifty-five years ago, somewhere between the space flights of Alan Shepherd and John Glenn. But I am fairly certain that I was not able to play "Mary Had a Little Lamb" as well as this volunteer did- after only 20 minutes.

Bill used no music, nothing about the musical scale or notes. That was not because the volunteer already knew music. If so, Bill would have said what notes were being played so the student could have a frame of reference. He was not told, "Now you are going to play a 'G', second line of the staff."

He did start out by telling the student that it was all about the "air." He did not even have the volunteer buzz the mouthpiece, an act of heresy to many band directors or teachers. He simply demonstrated what to do and then told the student to do it.

I'm not going to go into any greater detail about the specifics of what Bill did, which I realize will disappoint any of us who may want a step-by-step description of what to do in what order. I will not do that for the simple reason I can't. I can't because first of all, my notes were not clear about what he did. I was more interested in watching and only recorded thoughts, not the steps. The second reason I can't is that Bill wouldn't tell me. I wrote him an email, and true to his style of teaching didn't give me any such plan for instruction. Instead, he wrote:

> Everything I did was in reaction to the student. It's all about under-standing the concept then articulating/communicating in your own words and style. IMO this can't be expressed in the written word and is the reason Mr. Adam never wrote a book. Imagine the master in *Zen In the Art of Archery* writing a book on his methods. I don't think so.

As usual, Bill nudged me into thinking about this in a different way. First, it is not about the method, it is always about the student. A good teacher in a situation like that must be ready to pay attention to the student and what the student needs. The good teacher must be able to read the student's responses and adapt to what is needed at the moment. Not that the teacher doesn't have lesson plans or a toolbox filled with ideas and methods. The good teacher knows which to use and when and is also on the lookout for new ways as new students are encountered.

Teaching is communication. So is learning. It is the receiving and reverse direction of communication.

With this in mind, I did look back in my notes to see what I could now learn from the little bit I did write down. What I found was two things.

We have taught trumpet as if the student is deaf. For example, we tell them to push the 1st valve and you will get "F". It becomes a technical exercise as opposed to musical. They learn that if you push this you will get what you are looking for. We don't pay attention to what it sounds like. Bill had the student sing the note in imitation of what he did. With that we begin to enter into the realm of music and not technique. What does it sound like, is as important as what valves do I have to push to get that note on the page. Reading the music is very important (Doh!) but so it what we hear. We are not deaf.

I am sure we have experienced this when working on a scale. We push the wrong valve and the sound is wrong. We know by hearing that we have played a note that is not normally a part of that scale at that point. (Note that I didn't say it was a wrong note! It just doesn't fit what the scale sounds like.) We don't know it because our brain tells us we pushed the wrong valves, we know it because it didn't sound right. It is important to try to develop that sound awareness from the very start or build it back if you have lost it. Playing music is more than just the right fingering, it is the sound! Which brings me to the other thing I learned from Bill's demonstration lesson:

Buzzing isn't what makes the sound- it's the air. From the very beginning Bill talked about "air". He used various techniques to have the student experience "air" including submersing the bell in a bucket of water for the student to see when his air flow changed. Can you feel the difference, not just see it in the water? That's also at least part of the reasoning behind the Bill Adam technique of playing through the lead pipe without the tuning slide in place. It's about the sound of the air. We learn by listening when the air is going well, when it is centered. You can hear the difference. We then learn to play that way with the tuning slide back in. I do notice I have a better tone in practice when I start with the lead pipe air exercise!

I had a quick example of how this works the other week in band rehearsal. I was talking with one of the other trumpet players about some of Mr. Adam's ideas and things I have learned from Bob Baca and Bill Bergren. I mentioned the lead pipe air exercise. He asked me, "What does that do?" So I showed him. I didn't tell him. I pulled the tuning slide out and played. I had not warmed up yet so the sound wasn't centered. I showed what I knew how to do. I explained what I was doing. Then I did it one more time. "The goal," I said, "is to have that same air no matter where on the scale you are."

The result of all this in particular is back to the three things we should always have:

> Great not good sound
> Great not good rhythm and
> Great not good ears.

Listen, imitate, put it together. The sound will follow if you listen, imitate, and put it together.

Those are the basics, and I have a hunch that no matter where we are on the skill development journey, we will be able to learn from them. Oh, and a reminder to myself that if Bill does this demonstration at this summer's trumpet workshop, I will record it.

That's not all I got from Bill's brief note. But that will take another whole post, so I will save that for next week.

Chapter 2.23

The Magic in the Music

I said last week that, as usual, Bill Bergren had opened a new thought pattern for me in my post on his teaching a non-trumpet player how to play. Here, again, is his response from last week:

Everything I did was in reaction to the student. It's all about understanding the concept then articulating/communicating in your own words and style. IMO this can't be expressed in the written word and is the reason Mr. Adam never wrote a book. **Imagine the master in Zen In the Art of Archery writing a book on his methods. I don't think so.**

I bolded the part I want to talk about this week. It is, in essence, a challenge to the written word as the sole way of learning how to do something. He mentioned an older book: *Zen in the Art of Archery* that was written in the early 1930s and updated in the late 1940s. It is the first of many books that have taken the teachings of Zen and applied them to any number of other activities. The classic from the 1970s, *Zen and the Art of Motorcycle Maintenance* was one of the more famous. Such books, to oversimplify them, are philosophical discussions based on or around particular subjects. They take "Zen" ideas and apply them to life.

Here's Wikipedia's description of the archery book:

[German philosophy professor Eugen] Herrigel has an accepting spirit towards and about unconscious control of outer activity Westerners heretofore considered wholly to be under conscious-waking control and direction. For example, a central idea in the book is how through years of practice, a physical activity becomes effortless both mentally and physically, as if our habit body executes complex and difficult movements without conscious control from the mind.

Herrigel describes Zen in archery as follows:

"(...) The archer ceases to be conscious of himself as the one who is engaged in hitting the bull's-eye which confronts him. This state of unconscious is realized only when, completely empty and rid of the self, he becomes one with the perfecting of his technical skill, though there is in it something of a quite different order which cannot be attained by any progressive study of the art (...)" (https://en.wikipedia.org/wiki/Zen_in_the_Art_of_Archery)

It is a short book and an easy read, unless you want to allow it to work on you. Then slow down and listen to it. I could do a number of posts on what I wrote down, but let me take a few ideas.

Part of what this boils down to is that learning "technique" is not always enough. For the archery master Herrigel studied under to have given him a step-by-step description of the way to become proficient at archery, would not have produced a master. For us to simply know that pressing a certain valve or combination of valves produces a certain note does not make a good trumpet player. The "inner game" books by Timothy Gallwey and others present the same ideas in a different form. But I want to stick with the "Zen" idea for this post to give a slightly different perspective from the inner game. This perspective may actually prod us further into being less conscious about our playing and more in-tune (intentional phrase!) with ourselves, our playing, and our fellow musicians.

So, what might "Zen and the Art of Music" be like? I found this description from David Michael Wolff, founder and conductor of the Carolina Philharmonic with that very title:

Music has a certain magic to it, a magic infused with zen. If you start to see the energy underneath music instead of dwelling on the surface emotion, you see that lines of energy and rhythm guide the architecture... How can you work with the flow of energy instead of against it? Just as a great martial artist can defeat the opponent using his own energy, so a zen music master learns to bend musical energy to his will, or better, ride it effortlessly by bending himself to the will of music. -Link-(http://www.carolinaphil.org/zen-and-the-art-of-music/?author=5696a86bd82d5e5b49759d51)

Bend yourself as the musician to the will of music. But in order to do that you must also "see" the energy in the music and that there is a structure, an architecture to the energy and rhythm. Somewhat like the inner game except this clearly says that there is more to being a good musician than getting "self-one" to be quite so "self-two" can get in the flow. It is saying that together, self-one and self-two can get in the low with that is already in the music waiting to be released. Yes, self-one will attempt to shoe-horn and pressure the music to fit its ideas, but sooner or later self-two will say "Relax! Hear and feel the power underneath!

Personally, I love the idea in this. I know there is "magic" in the music that is waiting for the musician to share it. The technical notes on the page or the strategies we learned in Arban's or Clarke are the starting points, but they only work on the surface. They help us feel familiar with the technical aspects of playing, but if they don't move us to hear the music energy, we will simply be playing the notes and not the music itself. I find that exciting. That means for me that in each piece of music I am working on, whether an etude in Charlier or an old band favorite for a concert, there is something more than meets the eye. We can call it the architecture, but that is made up of the rhythms and energy connecting with us.

Bach is one of the best examples in this for me. It is precise, almost mathematically correct. It is some of the most "logical" music ever written. But that isn't why Bach's music remains as unique as it is. Logic and precision can get pretty boring. If you hear the "metronome" in the performer's head, you know the performer has missed the point of the music. But listen… there's the amazing love of Anna Magdelena in the notes or the soaring craving for God that sings like heaven in Bach's variations on what we know as "The Passion Chorale." Yes, it can take technical skill (i.e., years of practice) to get that into a performance, but it's the emotions that make it a real musical event.

How do we achieve this Zen-like attitude?

Many of these are what you would expect.

You have to know your instrument, its feel, its balance in your hands, the way it centers your sound. Think playing the lead pipe along for this. That's one of the ways we begin to connect with our instrument.

You have to build your strength or endurance. Think long tones centered and improving as you feel the center.

You have to breathe with your instrument and the music. Think long tones and the Clarke exercises.

You have to practice. Herrigel is told by the Master, "Don't ask- practice." There are aspects of practice that are important like singing the piece, playing it slow enough to know what the notes feel and sound like, recording yourself, listening to other recordings. All of these are not a prescription to Zen and music, they are simply part of the practice. A classic Zen idea is to realize that you will know it's happening when it is time. Until then wait with patience- and keep practicing.

One way I have found that seems to be working for me is moving beyond simply playing scales to improvising on them. I have never been able to improvise, except when singing along with a song, alone, in my car. I am a jazz lover and am empowered by listening to it. Since Shell Lake's Adult Big Band Workshop two years ago I have been moving toward experiencing what improvising is life. I went through the technical stuff of scales- major, seventh, and minor. They began to feel familiar under my fingers. I was accomplishing several of the things I mentioned above- the instrument, endurance, breathing- technical skills. I just kept practicing. I had difficulty playing with the Aebersold CDs, so I stopped trying. It wasn't time. I did slightly better with the iReal Pro app on my iPhone, but still struggled.

Then, one day, it was time. As I finished playing through my scales one afternoon I decided to play around with the scale. I started improvising. By ear. (It's amazing how much faster we can play a scale or a riff if we don't have to look at the music. I was flabbergasted!) I played with scales and chord arpeggios. I then added a structure of rhythm. Finally, I started adding structure of chord changes. I started working on 8- and 16-bar blues changes, then some ii-V7-I changes. I started playing them in different keys. I wanted to look in a mirror to make sure that it was still me playing the horn. The freedom that gave me was nothing short of miraculous. I started composing melodies across the changes. Sure, they were very elementary and quite dull, but I was doing something different.

I was experiencing the Zen.

I then started applying all this to a song I have been wanting to arrange for our quintet- the folk song *Sloop John B*. I worked it out by ear, then I started playing with it, checking different rhythms and chord changes, descants and the like. All by ear. I began to experience the Zen of this song. I then heard new things that I could play and ways to truly move beyond simple improvisation to some slightly more interesting variations. As I did this the power and energy of the song became apparent. I could feel it in my horn and embouchure. (I know that anyone who loves technical stuff will probably give up at this point. That's okay. It is working for me!)

Each time I play through the song now, I get a different insight into its structure and energy. I am almost ready to be getting the composing part going. Because I know the music, the song's Zen, it will be more interesting than if I had simply done some technical study and fit that to the song.

Be careful, of course, that you don't get into some bad habits. It could be easy to get used to doing things some incorrect ways. More on that in another post. For this week, Zen works. Go with the musical flow- it's energy and rhythm, its architecture and texture.

Bill, as usual, you've done it again.

And as usual, thanks.

Chapter 2.24

Goals!!

I forget where I recently saw this, so I can't give attribution, although a Google search turns up lots of others who use it. But this was quite a wake-up when I saw it:

- I don't know about you, but I don't wake up in the morning with aspirations for mediocrity.

Maybe some mornings I wake up and don't want to do what is needed to avoid mediocrity, and other days I'm just fine with being average as days go. Yet when it comes to a lot of different aspects of life, mediocrity is not what most of us want to settle for. So why do we?

Some of it goes back to what I said about grit a few weeks ago.

- We lose interest,
- don't have the energy, or
- believe we can't be anything but mediocre.

- Since I can't be as great as Miles or Maynard why bother at all?

I will end up being satisfied to be as mediocre as… well, as mediocre as me.

I return to something Bill Bergren emailed me a few months ago that I didn't use at the time:

> Tiger Woods tells us we should never have to use more than 80% of our capacity when striking the golf ball. The same goes for playing the trumpet. This means your ability must be at a very high level to allow for that 20% buffer.

When I read that I realized why I had been stuck for so many years at what I am today calling "mediocre." My capacity, let's call it overall ability wasn't that great. I never practiced regularly. That began to change when I started playing in three different groups and was playing more often. I was still mediocre, but less so. I was on the right track. I had no buffer like Tiger talks about because all I ever did was play when I needed to. My ability and endurance both ran out before the end of the rehearsal or gig.

Which fits what Bill said in the paragraph following the one above.

Tiger also tells us that the number of hours at the practice range or playing practice rounds far exceeds the time actually playing golf. This is true of any sport...........and music.

Makes sense, of course. If I can't play more than 25 or 30 minutes, I'm not going to make it through a sixty- or ninety-minute gig. Fitting in just enough time to sort of work on the tougher passages won't help a great deal. I remember the years in the summertime municipal band. At the start of the season, I was lucky to get through the rehearsal. With a few days a week of working on those tough passages I could soon move up to at least getting through rehearsal. (The breaks when the director worked with the woodwinds helped.) By the end of the summer, I could play through the whole concert, but I didn't have a lot left over. There was improvement (in endurance) but I didn't know that it was still just mediocre. In order to get that 20% buffer, I needed to practice far more than playing the gig.

How much time is needed? Perhaps 20% more? But I have no answer to that. I did notice something in the book on Zen and the Art of Archery that I mentioned last week. Eugen Herrigal reports simply being told by the archery Master,

"Don't ask- practice."

There are aspects of practice that are important like singing the piece, playing it slow enough to know what the notes feel and sound like, recording yourself, listening to other recordings. All of these are not a prescription to Zen and music, they are simply part of the practice. A classic Zen idea is to realize that you will know it's happening when it is time. Until then wait with patience- and keep practicing.

Again, last fall I adapted some of what Bill Bergren wrote to me with the deliberate practice ideas from the book, *Peak: Secrets from the New Science of Expertise* by Anders Ericsson and Robert Pool.

- Deliberate practice is focused. Students must give it their full attention.
- Deliberate practice involves feedback. Immediate, specific feedback on where students are falling short is vital.
- Deliberate practice requires a teacher
- Deliberate practice requires leaving one's comfort zone. If students aren't pushing themselves beyond what is comfortable and familiar, they will not advance.
- Deliberate practice requires specific goals aimed at target performances
- Deliberate practice builds on mental representations.

I have paid little attention to #5 on the list:

Deliberate practice requires specific goals aimed at target performances.

Last year in the first year of the Tuning Slide I took a shot at this idea. I have never been good at that type of planning in my practice regimen. Since reading the ideas in Peak and its explanation of deliberate practice I have spent some time thinking more about the idea of goals and plans. I'm still growing in that area, but I have learned some things. Well, one thing for sure:

Figure out what you want to do (the target performance) and then plan ways to do it (specific goals).

What I have discovered over the past two years of this head-long leap into becoming a trumpet player that isn't mediocre is to have a routine. Do it regularly. Daily is the goal. That's where we have to start. When I made that a goal, it actually happened. Doh!

But then we have to be deliberate about it. We don't just pick up the horn and start playing anything we feel like playing. A routine of long-tones, scales, Clarke studies, etc. Those remain the basics. Doing them daily is a key **goal**. I didn't even know I needed to do them or that if I did, I would improve as much as I have.

Ask questions of your teachers and/or mentors about what you need to be doing. Then do what they suggest. Get a mentor or teacher and pay attention. That is the **goal. That's where the goal begins to get specific, about you and what you need.**

Read, research, and listen. In so doing you can find out what you want to improve. That's the goal. Then put it into practice. That's the goal. For example, I have always (!) wanted to be better at jazz improvising. I bought several of the Aebersold books (https://www.jazzbooks.com/), messed around with them for a very short period and then set them aside. "I guess that won't happen," was my response. What I didn't realize was that before I would be able to do that I needed the basics. After the first goals above became reality I started reading more, researching more, listening more. I achieved a decent basic mastery of the 12 major keys. Now I had learned more of the language I needed. **Goal!**

Recently I came across a simple exercise on basic licks that can help get the feel of jazz under my fingers. Simple **goal** Practice one of these a day for six-days, in all 12 major keys. (Right there I would have set it aside if I hadn't had the other goals earlier.) Then on the seventh day- don't rest- but play through all of them. Doing that is a **goal**. Today is the seventh day and I am looking forward to seeing how well this fits together. (See Learn Jazz Standards. (https://www. learnjazzstandards.com/blog/6-patterns-for-major-scales/) And- I am doing all this without written music, which was another goal in this past six-months- to work on my listening- and translating what I hear into music.

I am amazed some days at how long it has taken me (55 years?) to learn this about my trumpet playing. Fortunately, I knew some of this from my vocation outside of music. I would have starved to death a long time ago if I hadn't. Applying it to my music has been the extra added value!

Again, this isn't rocket science:

Set **goals**- figure out what you want to do and then plan ways to do it.

Of course,

then do it!

Chapter 2.25

Watching and Listening

Sometime it is just neat to be in the audience when music is being made. Part of the discipline of being a musician is to go and hear others playing in performance. I have had a number of opportunities to do that over the past few months and have come away with some insights that I hope I can apply to my own public performance. In particular I have had the time to hear some types of music that I don't personally play. When I go to a concert where I am hearing different types of music, I kind of mentally prepare myself with five questions. These help me focus on the music, not so much from a technical aspect but from the perspective of a music fan. These questions:

- What's familiar?
- What's different?
- What's new and interesting?
- What do I like about it?

What can help me in my own playing and performance?

The most interesting concert for me was the Russian String Orchestra in a relatively small (500 seat) venue. It wasn't quite like sitting by the stage in a club environment, but it was close. I very seldom get to hear strings in person. And even less do I get to hear "just strings" in person. Strings have a unique and wondrous sound in an orchestral setting. I can still remember the first time I heard an orchestra in person. I was 22 and just about to graduate from college. I spent the summer in Austria and there I heard a chamber orchestra perform in a local cathedral. I was swept away. The sound of such an ensemble is hard to match.

The Russian String Orchestra consists of 16 string players, violin to double bass. My first thought was, "Gee, that's about how many we have in our big band." But there wasn't a trumpet, trombone, saxophone - or amplifier- in sight. Which is the first thing that caught me up short; this is a 100% acoustic performance. There's no manipulation of the sound, what is there is what you hear. It is not a "large" sound, but it does get through. It has an amazing range of dynamics. The quiet subtlety of a pianissimo section is almost breathtaking in its simplicity- and wonder. That they can easily move from that to a fortissimo that brings thunderstorms to mind is even more amazing. The ability to have that kind of control over one's instrument is almost miraculous.

Which is the first thing I took away from the concert. The hours of practice it takes to be that controlled in your music is critical, as I have talked about before. But to hear the results of that practice shows what a great gift it can be to the audience. Trumpet players aren't traditionally known for their subtlety. Maybe it is worth working on that. Yes, it is difficult in a big band of brass and woodwinds to get that, but the result- for the audience- is priceless. Music is not just blasting away or developing high screaming notes or even a fast chromatic run. The silence between the notes may be just as important, which is where the subtlety can be born.

The concert itself was purely "classical" string music-style. No pop numbers adapted for strings. It was the real deal. And, no surprise, it used all the same notes that every other band I play in uses. The rich variety of music available to us to hear and play is remarkable. On top of that, it also follows many of the same rules that I have been working on with my jazz improvisational learning, and most certainly what I find in Arban's, Clarke, or Charlier etudes.

The second thing I did was I listened more closely to get the groove of the music. I could pick out certain musical progressions that I am trying to become intimate with- variations on the ii-V7-I cadence found in so many jazz and popular numbers were there. So was the eight-bar phrasing at times, giving me the movement, I could flow with. Hearing the music being moved around the different instruments, allowing each section and, on one piece, each member, to show off their virtuosity was entrancing. I moved with the music- and it became even more alive.

Again, how much work goes into that? These musicians were more than proficient- they were professionally expert! Part of what they have done is to learn the music, feel the rhythm, and then allow the music to transfer through them and their instrument to their fellow musicians and to the audience. That is back to the control of their instrument (remember self-one) allowing the natural development of the music to intuitively come out (remember self-two.) But what I took away for me, beyond the practice and "Inner Game" thoughts, is again those three things we have talked about before:

1. Every time you play you have a great- not a good- sound.
2. You have great- not good- rhythm.
3. You have great- not good- ears to hear the sound.

All three of those come together with what I was hearing.

The third thing that I have learned to watch when musicians are performing is how do they look? Are they just doing a job, or are they interested, engaged, even excited? I had seen that in a concert of Irish music and dancing the week before. Those young people were remarkable in their raw energy and their ability to harness it for the show. They were not polished like, say, *Riverdance*. But they were every bit as good. They were excited by the performance and the engagement with us the audience.

I saw that same kind of excitement with the Russian Strings. They were having fun. Being in such a small venue I could easily watch their faces, their eyes, the movement of their bodies. I saw them look across the orchestra and smile when someone did a great job. I watched them lean into the music and get ready for the next section that was important to them personally. I saw the little communications that passed information from one to the other. They were intensely involved in the music, they liked the music, and they were excited to be able to play it.

Part of that comes from their incredible intimacy with the music and the way they have learned to listen and work with each other. They may all be highly skilled, but they clearly know at this point in their careers that they need each other. I hope they never lose that. Part of it, too, is that they, like the Irish group the week before, truly like what they are doing. They get that from their conductor. He loved directing the music; he loved the opportunities this orchestra gives young people; he is excited by sharing it with us in the audience, even when the microphone didn't work as well as he wanted it to. He was contagious- the orchestra caught it. The orchestra was contagious- and we caught it.

It was a great evening of music. But it was also a great evening of learning for me and a reminder of why I do what I do with my music. Yes, it feels great to be able to build my chops and, for example, move through 12 major scales with little effort, or (Mr. Baca, Steve, and Warren take note) regularly hitting that high "C" and "D". But if that is all I do, it will be nothing more than a selfish endeavor. It is in the performance that the true magic of music does its work. Therefore:

- Deliberate practice to be able to give better performances. Develop the breadth and subtlety of the music.
- Maintain the interest in finding new ways to be excited by what I am doing.
- Stay engaged with the music and the groove in performance so it can fit together.
- Put all these together on the bandstand or concert stage.
- Be contagious and let the audience catch it.

Chapter 2.26

Anxiety

I've written about performance anxiety before- and my 45-year battle with it. Last May in year one I described what I have always considered my initial bout with it on a Memorial Day over 50 years ago. (See the chapter "Losing My Mojo.") Throughout this year I have continued to work on it and I am finding myself improving. I have sorted out some of the other issues like perfectionism, making a fool of myself, worry about what people will think, letting myself down, letting the other musicians down, letting the audience down, and on and on. No wonder I get performance anxiety- that's a lot of heavy-duty baggage I carry around to every performance.

One thing I have taken note of is that performance anxiety does not generally happen in rehearsals, although there have been exceptions. That usually happens in the larger groups when all of a sudden (as if I didn't know it was coming? Right!) I have a part that stands out, and usually in a final rehearsal more so than earlier. In fact, most of the time in rehearsal my self-improvement plan of the last two years has shown positive results for me. I am generally pleased with how things continue to fall into place. I usually leave a practice session feeling fulfilled and relaxed.

But some of the signs of the anxiety still show up in the performances- overly concerned with what's going to happen, dry mouth, some nervousness, the feeling down deep somewhere that I'm about to blow it- again. It's not happening as much as it used to, but it's still there and I continue to tweak my methods.

Looking back in my notes from the Shell Lake Trumpet Workshop the other day I found this list of ways to deal with it. I don't remember (and didn't note) if this was from one particular lecture at the workshop or a combination of things from different places. If I am neglecting to give someone credit, my apologies. Let me know and I will give you the props for it. In any case, here is the basic note with my updates and thoughts about each as I have worked on it this past year.

To deal with performance anxiety

- *Put performance in perspective*

One performance in terms of whole career? It's a lot smaller deal than I am making it. Not to mention that I am not doing this as a career. In the while scheme of things any given performance is not all that earth-changing, especially at my level. Yes, there are performances that do make a difference, but most of them aren't. By experiencing performing without anxiety, I can learn that I am able to perform better than I thought.

- *Overly concerned about what other people think of you?*

They probably don't even notice when things aren't perfect. I have done some improvising- as part of the big band and at a jam session. I am looking to do more of that to help me continue to gain the skills of listening and translating it into the language of the trumpet. I am learning that when I do that, people are usually on my side and want me to do well. No one is sitting there saying, "I really want Barry to mess this up!"

- *Breathe. Be in the moment. You won't be thinking ahead or what other people, or whatever*

I talk a lot about this- and can utilize it in many ways, except on stage! On stage it seems to enhance the concerns and anxiety instead of easing them. That probably means I need to practice my mindfulness with less depending on it. It does work, but it can't if I focus my breathing on how I'm about to mess up. Relax- and tell Self One to just be quiet!

- *See that we are taking the emotion coming from the music, not the other way around.*

We are the conduit. Let the music do the talking. Let the horn speak. This is part of the focus we seek in our practice. Did I say practice? I know that too often when practicing something more difficult or a solo part, I tend to look too much on the technical quality of what I am doing. By the time I get to a concert or gig the technical part shouldn't be a problem. I should be moving well beyond that in my practice room and into the groove, emotion, rhythm, and style of the piece. In rehearsals I should be listening to how my part fits into the greater whole. Whether it is a concert band solo or improvising in a big band piece, I need to know the emotion of the music... and all music isn't stuck in my emotion of anxiety.

- *Think like someone else.*

Like Miles or Maynard? Well, maybe, but in reality, what I almost have to do is begin to think like a person who can play the part- and play it well. I am not the bumbling musician that self-one is convinced I am. I know what I am doing- again, especially if I have given practice the time and energy it needs.

- *You are a person who plays trumpet, not a trumpet player who happens to be a person*

It's like going in a circle- I am back to the first of these ideas. My personal dignity, worth, or self is not the trumpet, t's in being who I am. THAT is what I want to share through the horn. I am learning how to do that, which makes it easier to put the anxiety aside.

- Have fun practicing!

I do this because I enjoy it. I need to enjoy the music I make in practice as well. That is where self-one learns to trust self-two. Maybe I need to stop the tweaking of my plan to get over performance anxiety- and just learn to do it. No, not learn to do it- just do it. And that takes the ability to focus. We'll get to that next week.

Chapter 2.27

Focus

Last week I talked about anxiety, specifically performance anxiety and some ways to deal with it. My last point in that post was:

- **Have fun practicing!**

  I do this because I enjoy it. I need to enjoy the music I make in practice as well. That is where self-one learns to trust self-two. Maybe I need to stop the tweaking of my plan to get over performance anxiety- and just learn to do it. No, not learn to do it- just do it. And that takes the ability to focus.

I realized as I was summing up things last week that performance anxiety is enhanced, if not caused, by distraction or lack of focus. When I am "working on" "dealing with" my anxiety I am NOT focused on the music. Distraction causes me to lose my ability to stay on task- even a task that is simple and deeply ingrained. I found that happen several times last week when I was practicing scales sitting on the balcony. It has been my favorite place to practice this winter- the Gulf of Mexico, the birds, the wonder of the sky and beach all add a sense of peace.

But only if I don't focus on them.

So I was running through one of the basic, level one scales, you know, Bb and Eb concert. Most of us can probably do them in our sleep. But not as well if you get sidetracked by something around you-

Hey, look at that pelican..

What a beautiful sky it is today..

Or, ... well you get the picture. As soon as even the simplest thought entered consciousness, I would miss notes or my fingers would get flubbed up or I would forget where I was in the scale.

That is a major problem of mine. I have never been diagnosed as ADD, but I sure can be easily...

Squirrel!

...distracted.

I have improved in my performance distractibility. For one I have a pair of reading glasses that focus best at about the distance of the music stand. I can't see the movements in the audience as easily. (Chalk up one good thing for age!) I have also learned how to stay more focused on the director from peripheral vision alignment. That way I can stay focused on the music in front of me and not get lost when moving from looking at the music, then to the director and back again.

The next step in this process is to deal with focus in practice. That brings me back to

- planning,
- goal setting,
- being intentional in my schedule,
- keeping a journal,
- recording myself, and
- using a metronome.

Here is where I still struggle. I have improved in the first three, but need work in the next three. I have a hunch that if I learn to increase my overall focus in practice, I will begin to find more of it in performance.

I can do it- any of us can. The best example of that may be that as Mr. Baca and others at the Shell Lake Trumpet Workshop have said:

If you have six-weeks to learn something- it will take you six weeks. If you have six days, you will be ready in six-days.

In the end that may be the best description of focus. Which is why goals, with timelines, are good ideas. They are self-imposed deadlines, yet not so demanding that you resent yourself for imposing them. All in all it is the working on those inner voices that can get us stuck- or soaring to new levels of ability. Focus is being able to sort out the helpful from the unhelpful, the reality from the fear, and learning how to be more in the present. John Raymond, trumpeter and Shell Lake Trumpet Workshop instructor wrote on this in a recent Facebook post.

About 15 years ago I came to New York for the first time. My dad managed to hook up a lesson with the great Vincent Penzarella and, while I didn't remember this until my dad reminded me a couple weeks ago, he dropped some HEAVY wisdom on me back then. It went something like this:

VP: "John, why are you here?"

JR: "I came out to NYC to check out some music schools and I thought this would be a great opportunity to learn from the best."

VP: "Great! Well, who's been your best teacher?"

JR: (most likely some immature response, although my first response was much better than I would've given myself credit for back then).

VP: "The best teacher you'll ever have is your own brain. You know when you are playing and are really in the zone, and then you miss a note. Your brain says "I messed up, oh no." The critical side of your brain can talk very loudly. But you can't be creative when your brain is critical."

"Your brain allows you to be critical or to be creative, but you can't do both at the same time. The critical side of your brain, especially for a perfectionist in music, can speak very loudly John. You need to learn how to manage that critical side. You are going to have to learn how to talk yourself out of that and let the creative side surface."

"Your number 2 best teacher is the music. Listen to the music, learn the music, respect the music, love the music, just as it is. It has been around for a lot of years for a reason."

I only wish I had the maturity back then to internalize all this.

Nevertheless, 15 years later and I can confidently say that these words are 100% ON POINT.

- John Raymond

Well, it is never too late to internalize it. That's what these posts and the whole Tuning Slide blog is about. It is moving forward, taking risks, pushing the envelope. It is finding new ways to be a better musician, a better person, and going to new places in our own experience.

Chapter 2.28

Rhythm

I spent some time at the American Jazz Museum in Kansas City yesterday. You walk into one section and you see a series of displays about the construction of jazz. They talked about the different instrument groups and what roles they play, but they made clear that there are three important elements to the "language of jazz:"

- Melody
- Harmony
- Rhythm.

A strong reminder on how all music is tied together. It doesn't matter what style of music you play; it will have its own language built on the foundational language of musical concepts and theory. It will build that language with the words, sentences, paragraphs and volume after volume of music on those three basic elements. Music can be said to be built by the interplay of melody, harmony and rhythm. Without getting too deep into music theory, periods, styles and all that (which is too western) let's link those three concepts.

Melody is:

the succession of single tones in musical compositions, as distinguished from harmony and rhythm. the principal part in a harmonic composition; the air. a rhythmical succession of single tones producing a distinct musical phrase or idea. (Dictionary.com)

Melody is what results from playing notes of different pitches - sometimes pitches can be repeated too - one after the other in an 'organised' way. Melodies are very distinguishable and are often singable. However, just the succession of pitches doesn't make a melody. Each note played has a duration. The relation between durations refers to rhythm.

But, before rhythm, let's talk about **pulse**. Like every living organism, music has a pulse - beats (like that of the heart). And although we not always hear it, it is always there. Do you remember when children learn to clap their hands to follow songs? There is a constant, implicit, beat that happens periodically. In some cases, it is in fact played by instruments. For example, in Australian aboriginal music it is often played by clap sticks.

But **rhythm** is not just a constant periodic beat. The beat or pulse is like its skeleton. Rhythm is how you inhabit the pulse. Rhythm is what results of combining notes of different durations, sometimes coinciding with the beat and sometimes not. For example, if you can notice in Reggae or Ska music, the guitar or keyboards most of the times play, at times, exactly opposite to the beat.

And, last but not least: **harmony**. Usually, melodies are not just played alone by a solo instrument or a group of instruments playing the same thing. Very frequently there are 'lead' instruments which play melodies (such as the voice, wind instruments, etc.) and, at the same time, others that accompany them doing something else. This relationship between different notes played at the same time is what we call harmony.

Sometimes this can be done by one instrument such as guitar or piano, but other times by several instruments (like brass ensembles). There are many types of relations between two or more notes played at the same time, but they can be classified into two main divisions: consonance and dissonance. (https://www.didjshop.com/BasicMusicalHarmony.html)

Again- it is in the interaction of these that what we call music is made. How do we learn to do that? Beyond the obvious issue of scales and listening to your music and those you are playing with; I have a hunch that rhythm is where we need to most practice. The "rhythm" section of any band needs to be solid or the group can't hold together. I have probably seen many a director work hard with the percussion section in order not to lose the beat, the pulse, the groove no matter what the style of music. Soloists who lose the feel of the music can potentially go off on their own leaving the band either far behind or a couple measures ahead. It is important to learn how to feel the music as much as it is to play it.

On the website, Learn Jazz Standards, they have a post about four ways to remain mediocre- number 3 is:

Ignore working on rhythm and time.

I find that a lot of mediocre jazz players spend the majority of their time working on their solos and navigating the vast array of harmonic structures jazz has to offer. Everyone wants to be a great soloist, and you will need to work on these things if you want to become one.

But it doesn't matter if you play the hippest lines or have the best technique if you don't groove. If your time feel is off, and you neglect all rhythmic studies you will be missing a key ingredient for jazz [or any musical] excellence.

When it comes down to it, if your music doesn't make people dance on some level, your music will feel off. It has to groove. Your single note lines need to groove, and your accompaniment needs to groove. If you rush or drag too much, it won't groove.

So, if you want to stay mediocre, ignore these things. But if you want to become an excellent jazz musician, start shifting some of your practice time from soloing to rhythm and time. (https://www.learn-jazzstandards.com/blog/learning-jazz/jazz-advice/4-ways-stay-mediocre-jazz-musician/?utm_content=bufferb31a4&utm_medium=so-cial&utm_source=facebook.com&utm_campaign=buffer)

People may not be dancing in the aisles at a concert band performance, but it must make them move internally. It must make them connect with some pulse. Rhythm is essential.

That's where the metronome can also come into play. I have previously indicated that I am not very good at working with a metronome. I hate being that regimented. I'd rather just go off and do it at whatever pace I want to, thank you very much! Which is why I am still just barely beyond mediocre in some things. My fear has always been that the metronome will make me too tied in a mechanical way to the beat. In the meantime, I haven't learned the discipline of the beat or learned how the song's groove moves. Until I learn that discipline I am not ready to move beyond it and bring it alive. Until I can play it smoothly while remaining disciplined, I haven't learned it.

Music is a living thing. Musicians make those broad kinds of statements all the time. But the pulse of music, the heartbeat is in the rhythm. When building athletic or physical endurance we start with a baseline. We often call that our "resting heart rate." That is exactly where we start with the music. The metronome is the guide to where to start. As time moves on, we begin in our physical training to pay attention to optimal heart rates for activities and to know when the rate has gotten out of the groove. Every athlete knows the signs of that-whether they name it as part of the rhythm or not. They know the groove that works for them. Once they get it, they can learn when and how to push it.

I am finally talking myself into using that metronome more often. Won't I be surprised when it actually works?

Chapter 2.29

Making Leaps

We don't move smoothly from one level of ability to next. Reading about quantum physics I realized that most of what happens in the world is not on a continuum. It may look like it, but it isn't. That's because we can't see the little things happening, down on the quantum level. The electrons, for example, move one energy level orbit to another in jumps. Discrete jumps. In-between they are nowhere. It is referred to as "discontinuous." In other words, a "leap" from one place to the next. Or maybe in a whole cloud of possibilities of all the things that could happen which in physics is known as a sum over paths.

I realized that this also explains some of what I have often noticed in my practicing and improvement as a musician. In summer band I used to notice somewhere around week 4 of rehearsals that my improvement slowed down and even regressed. This would happen just before I made a significant jump in my playing and skill. The first time it happened I almost quit the community band thinking that I was getting too old for that. (I was all of 38, and this was 30 years ago). Then, in a couple of weeks, in time for the second half of the summer band season, things would improve. When it happened again the next year, I figured it must be normal.

Recently I noticed, for example, that my upper register had begun to fall into place in ways I have never, repeat NEVER played before. I know I am approaching another jump in my skill. The next day I wasn't playing up there. Then I was. Or in my second set of practicing on a given day I was not able to do it as I had the day before. There is a discontinuity happening.

I am in that never-never land between skill levels. I'm not where I was, but I am not quite where I am going. I am in the cloud of possibilities. On any given day I might be approaching that new level and on the next, well, I'm barely where I was. When that happens, I get excited- it means things are changing. Here's what is happening as a way of illustrating:

It wasn't that long ago, within the past year, that the top of the staff was my comfortable limit. Yes, I could sort of hit above it, sometimes okay, usually not as well. My skill level was the top of the staff. Early this year I noticed I had become more comfortable all the way to line above the staff. Still not perfect, but changing. There was a new top.

Then three weeks ago, for the first time ever, I purposely went all the way to 5 notes above the staff. I could do it without too much problem. Sometimes. The old line was now comfortable. It was at that point, though, that I noticed a seeming regression in skill. For a few days I was barely getting to the comfortable line again. Instead of getting depressed, I got excited. The leap is beginning. In my old way of thinking I would have believed that I had reached the end of my skill. I even remember saying to one of the other big band and trumpet students (Jeff!) that I will never be getting up to the "E" let alone any higher. I don't believe that anymore. I heard the "E" come out of my horn and I know it will happen again.

Which brings me back to the listening part of music- having a "great ear." That doesn't just mean hearing when a note is right or wrong. It also means hearing the note before you play it. I used to take a quick break going up the scale as I went from "G" to "A" above the staff. I had to set myself to play it. I couldn't naturally hear it. In one book I saw online the general feeling of why many trumpet players can't play in the high register is that they aren't able to hear the notes up there. Once we can, we move toward playing it. Then, one day, the leap is made.

I do notice that the "leap" is not as fast as it used to be. I don't think it's because of anything I'm doing differently. I believe it has to do with the act that I am up in the upper range of the instrument. Some will argue, quite persuasively, that the range of the trumpet does go that high, but the fewer number of harmonics makes it a little more sensitive to smaller changes than lower on the instrument. As we move higher in the range, and build our own skills, embouchure, and endurance, the "center" of the trumpet scale moves upward on the staff. When you go to higher levels or greater extremes in any activity the progress doesn't change as quickly. But it still happens. As skill increases, so does the area of challenge.

As we come to the end of this second year of the Tuning Slide blog, I am aware of many of those leaps in my own playing. I am doing things I never thought possible- and know I am working toward more of them. These past two years have been a remarkable time for me as a person and as a musician. I have consistently called this blog reflections on music and life. They go together. When my life is in better balance and focus, so is my music. As my music focuses more, so does my life. What I learn in one, applies to the other. If there is one sentence that summarizes this second year it is:

How you do anything is how you do everything.

Keep at it. It's worth it

Postlude

Reflections of Music (and Life) In a Time of Pandemic

Where were you when the world shut down?

My wife and I were in Alabama with a couple weeks left in our annual snowbird time. As we watched the news and followed the experts, we decided it would be best to cut it short and head home to Minnesota. We have spent the year being safer at home. As I worked on writing and reading, figuring out retirement, and practicing my trumpet, I came to realize that much of what I had written in the earlier printing of this book has helped me get through the past year. When I decided to publish it under a new title, I also knew I had to add a few posts about what that all means.

Here are three new posts. The first was written in August 2019. We had no idea of the pandemic looming on our doorstep. The second was written as we headed home in March 2020. Uncertainty was a word to describe what we felt. The third has been written at the one-year anniversary of the trip home.

They bring this book to an end. They sum up how what I learned with the mindful mastery of my trumpet playing has applied to my life.

Postlude #1

A Letter to Mr. Baca

Originally posted August 12, 2019

Anyone who stops learning is old, whether at twenty or eighty.

—Henry Ford

As I started the fifth year of the Tuning Slide Blog in August 2019, I took some time to think about what I have experienced and learned since that first August at Shell Lake Trumpet Workshop.

I have decided to put it into the form of a letter to Bob Baca, the director of the workshop and my main mentor these past four years. I am not ignoring the other faculty and people at home who have been part of this journey with me. Together they have helped me implement the ideas and more to where I am today!

Hi Bob,

Well, I missed the trumpet week at Shell Lake this year. It was a tough decision, but I have an opportunity to do some different kind of stretching in my musicianship and I'm taking it. As I told you I will be going to an adult concert band camp in Door

County in a couple weeks and couldn't swing both this year. But more on that later in the year. Instead, I want to summarize the many things that you (and the others) have helped me achieve.

What I have learned from these past 4 years:

1. Routine!

I remember from these years at Shell Lake that you and the faculty have often said that one plays a high C the same way one plays a low C. At first, I didn't understand, but I believed you and kept waiting for it to happen while doing what I needed to do. The time spent on playing the lead pipe and LONG TONES has paid off. Last year at the Brass Festival in North Carolina I found myself just playing what was on the page- and the notes came out. The answer to that was a routine. A routine that is regular and consistent.

2. The Basics.

I learned that if we don't continue to work on our skills, develop our tone, practice rhythms and etudes, we can become stale. Over these past four years I have been renewed in my skills, I have practiced and discovered more ways to speak the language of the trumpet and to put more style and tone and life into it. If I am to grow in any way in my abilities, I have to practice the basics- which you have taught me to do and then move into greater technical proficiency. All I wanted to do was be a better musician- and it has happened.

Many years ago, I was a first-chair, lead trumpet with whatever skills a high school senior could have in1965. I learned the importance of being a section player and discovered all kinds of new techniques. I have never stopped playing, but in the past four years I went from "just playing" to "being musical". I would never have believed it when I left Shell Lake after that first camp in 2015. I have been amazed at what can happen- and yes, as I have said before, even an old dog can learn many, many new tricks.

Perhaps above all else I have discovered the absolute necessity of never leaving the basic behinds. The Bill Adam routine has taught me not to forget or neglect these basics on a daily basis. I play 10-20 minutes of long tones in various forms every day. It is the foundation. I play exercises in all 12 major keys; I go back and use the first Arban exercises regularly; I discovered that if I can hear it, I can play it. My fingers now move more fluidly through muscle memory and my ears hear more through aural memory.

3. Easy does it. Patience, slow down.

Don't force it; don't rush it. The secret to playing fast is to play slowly. Sometimes so slowly that you may not even recognize the tune. If it isn't working, go back to the basics behind it. So simple, yet so powerful.

4. You can skip a day but you'll never get it back

I have missed very few days over these last four years, mostly when I was recuperating from surgery and wasn't allowed to play. Once in a while I may take a day off because there was no way around it. More often I will do the basic long-tones and scales for 30 minutes. On most days I play and now I can play a lot.

5. Listen, listen, listen

Pay attention to yourself in your own practice and to those around you in rehearsal. We practice alone to get to know our part. We rehearse with others to know how our part fits in with the others.

6. The Inner Game- trust self 2

The Inner Game ideas have been around a while and they work. I have known them for years; now I know how to better utilize them and to trust me - Self 2- to do what I can do.

7. Play out. Just do it.

Some may think that a "timid trumpet player" is an oxymoron. Put me in a group or public performance and I would become a timid musician. What a waste. It is exciting. That doesn't mean to over-perform, be over loud or obnoxious. It means what it says- just do it!

8. Stretch outside the box

I know the importance of stretching one's skills. It is how we grow. What I have learned in these past four years has given me some directions on how to do that. I enjoy it too much now to even think of stopping.

9. It's at least 90% mental.

The basics of playing and performing music are the easy parts. Just keep practicing. This goes back to- and expands on the inner game. If you don't think you can do it- you won't be able to do it. But if you believe you can- you will- even if it takes months and years of practice.

10. Mindfulness

Mindfulness is the basis of a life of hope and growth. Being self-aware and then being aware of all that is around me and living within it- that's the ability to be mindful. It doesn't mean lack of growth or being content with just leaving things as they are. It means being attentive and, in my musicianship, knowing where I can go next.

That's what I have learned. Here is what I have received:

A. Play like you like it- and you will like playing.

This is perhaps best described in the meme: If you don't like playing long tones, you probably don't like playing trumpet. Really? Yep! It is fun to discover something new with different ways of doing long tones each day. I really like playing and it makes a real difference each day.

B. Confidence

Two weeks ago, at a community band rehearsal I had to play a solo part that I had never read before since the soloist wasn't able to be at that rehearsal. Then I had to play some upper register lines. Yep- I did both. Confidence has built. I don't get panicked when I see some of those notes or at a passage I would have backed off from before. Now, later this week, I will be attending that concert band camp where I have to audition. I am not the least bit afraid. Call out a major key- I can play any of the 12. Give me a sight-reading page- I know the basics. Am I nervous or anxious? Not anymore. Now I am excited.

C. Energy and excitement

What can I say? They sum up what I have been given. The other day I was feeling a little under the weather and restless, unable to find something to direct me. My wife looked at me and simply said, "Go play your trumpet. That always works."

And it did.

Thank you, Bob and the Shell Lake Trumpet Workshop. You have given me one of the greatest boosts of the past 30 years.

Crazy! Crazy good!

[Between that post and the one that follows everything was normal. We had a normal Fall season, celebrated Christmas, then packed up and headed south as snowbirds to coastal Alabama. My music increased in new areas. For the first time I played as part of a contemporary worship band at the local Gulf Shores United Methodist Church. That kicked my musical skills into new areas- like working from chord and lead sheets. The Baldwin County Pops band concert was another year of good people and good music. Everything was normal. Until overnight it wasn't.]

Postlude #2

As the Pandemic Began

Originally written on March 16, 2020

This will be our reply to violence: to make music more intensely, more beautifully, more devotedly than ever before.

— Leonard Bernstein

This quote was originally written after the death of President John F. Kennedy in 1963. It was a time of uncertainty and chaos, fear and grief. As I sat down to write I realized that I cannot write what I had intended to write about. First, I had to clear my mind of all the things running around in there in the midst of the current time of uncertainty and pandemic and fear.

These are times like none other we have seen in many years. Perhaps the closest we can come to it in the last fifty years is September 11, 2001. Suddenly things were different. It felt like the world of order and sanity was under attack. These things that are this disruptive of life as we have known it don't happen often, but they are gut wrenching when they do.

This afternoon (March 16, 2020) I did a simple shopping trip. We are on our way back home to Minnesota from Alabama, our time cut short by the exponential growth of the virus worldwide and the cultural and societal changes that are coming along. It may be that we will never again see the world as we did just a few short weeks ago. Churches, schools, gyms, concerts, band rehearsals, coffee shops, movie theaters, fast food restaurants are all different today. As I drove through the small Missouri city where we are staying this evening, I saw the impact with empty parking lots and empty shelves in Walmart. And not just the hand-sanitizer and toilet paper. Food aisles are empty, too. Over the counter medication shelves are less than fully stocked.

Then I see an amazing story from Italy where they have been in lockdown for a number of days. The streets are empty. But there's a trumpet player standing on his balcony playing. There are neighbors singing with each other. Music was a source of strength for those people as they shared their time and talent, even in the midst of the chaos and uncertainty.

Take time to listen to music these next weeks. Extend that listening into the months after that. Turn this time of fear and chaos into a time when the depths of our humanity can be touched with hope and peace. Those of us who play in musical groups, it doesn't matter what the style or genre, start thinking about what and how you can make a difference when the curfews come down and the lock-downs open up. Listen and research and practice. Take time away from the daily chaos of the news and retreat into music or reading or meditating or taking a walk if you can. Find the music in your own heart and enhance it.

We may not know where all this will lead; We can know that if we follow the music of the heart and soul- each of our individual hearts and souls- we will find the sound and the harmony, the rhythm and the style that can bring greater hope to the world. Those of us who are musicians have a wondrous gift to share. May we take this time to discover how to expand it for the good of ourselves, our families and friends, and wherever we may go.

I guess I needed to talk about this- to adjust my personal tuning slide, to remind myself of why I am doing this and how important it is to me. Now I'm going to listen to some music, read a while, and do it again tomorrow.

Postlude #3

A Year of Safer at Home

Written March 2021

Musicians don't retire; they stop when there's no more music in them.

-Louis Armstrong

Today is a day like most of the last 365-plus days. I will spend most of it in my "office" writing, surfing the Internet, staring out the window. At some point in the day, usually mid-late-afternoon, or after supper, I will look next to my chair and see the trumpet and think, "Time to practice?"

Yes, it is a question. My response depends on nothing in particular. It is more a rhetorical question than a real one. The answer should always be "Yep!" Even when it isn't. As on most days since the journey of this book began in 2015, the answer is to pick it up and start warming up.

In many ways I am lucky to be somewhat of an introvert. The past twelve months proved that as my wife and I have managed quite well at home, even without our annual winter in Alabama. In this year I first had to face full-retirement, meaning a reevaluation of what I am doing with my life. That took a couple months of readjusting the compass of my life and seeing fewer people. I continued to practice every day.

Then I was faced with the loss of all performances and rehearsals of the bands and quintet I have been a part of. That meant less outside contact with others beyond my wife. I continued to practice every day.

I learned how to connect with people via Zoom. That kept the outside contacts alive and actually increased my contacts far beyond the local face-to-face friends locally. I was now actually reconnected with people I had not spent a lot of time with over the past ten years due to distance. I continued to practice every day. Without any gigs, I did a self-evaluation and decided to do some intense and focused practice on things that were the weaker parts of my ability.

I attended a couple music Zooms, including with Bob Baca and the people from the Shell Lake Trumpet workshop where all this started. It kept me focused and gave me ongoing inspiration. I still practiced as I had done for the past five years.

One of the big bands and the quintet began rehearsing outside in members' driveways. What a joy to be together again. I kept practicing.

Then came the surge in cases last fall, just as the groups would have needed to move inside. We had to stop. We have not been together now since October. I continued to practice most of the time.

Oh, did I say that out loud? I have to be honest and say that the absolute rule of practice every day didn't hold through the winter. Most weeks I still played five out of seven days. A couple different times I missed two days in a row. Once I missed three. I gave the usual excuses and rationalized that I was at a far better place overall in my playing so it wouldn't take much to get back to where I had been. As I would say that, I also could hear in the horn the truth of the familiar quote attributed to just about every musician who has ever been famous:

> If I miss one day's practice, I notice it. If I miss two days' practice, the critics notice it. If I miss three days' practice, the public notices it.

Meanwhile, in my broader world (the world of the pandemic), I had pivoted to a new, third career. I became a full-time author. I noticed that I was following the same path of mastery that I had followed in my trumpet playing over these years. Because of the intensity and learning curve, I needed to be even more intentional about developing that mastery as an author in a shorter time than I did with the trumpet.

What I did was start with knowing I could grow and change over these months. That was the growth mindset that improved my trumpet skills. I recognized the need for mentoring and coaching. I needed to be open to critical, supportive feedback. Since mastery is simply getting better at something you like, that's what I did. Practice, intentional direction, intense focus, critical feedback. I had learned the process of mastery from the trumpet; it took me to new places.

But this new career was taking time. I had been practicing, but not with the intentionality or direction I had been taught. I wasn't aware of needing it. Then, at the end of one particularly stressful day I looked down. There was the trumpet, calmly waiting for me. I picked it up.

I started with the good old long tones.

My body relaxed.

I went to chords.

My mind relaxed.

I did some simple etudes.

The stress lowered.

I played some jazz standards from the Fake Book.

I smiled.

I had not lost the meaning and purpose. "I like this!" I thought. All the basics came back when I began to focus again. But so did that awareness that through this music, or more broadly, through this work of mastery at music, which I love, came better skill and mastery about other things as well.

So, I re-read this book. I realized that the pivot I faced last year worked because I used the fundamentals that had kept me sober for over thirty years. I was following a tried-and-true path. I did the inner work of self-awareness and mindfulness that work:

- I did not depend on myself alone. That would only have reinforced my bad habits.
- I found groups to help with feedback and guidance.

- I did intentional planning and practice, guided by the course work of Self-Publishing School
- I had experiences of flow, the balance of challenge and skill that leads to growth.
- I listened to the wise mind- not the quick, emotional answer or the over analyzing of the logical answer.
- I moved, not stuck in "poor me" or blame, or even just staring out the window in mindlessness.

As I write this, the pandemic hasn't ended. We may never go back to all the ways it used to be. But in reality, with a growth mindset it never does. Instead with intentionality and mindful practice, we can move wherever we need to move, doing what the situation requires.

Two important lessons sum it up. It can be in the midst of a pandemic, or just getting through the average day. First, I remembered that if my playing and skills were seeming to lag for no apparent reason, it was probably a plateau, preparing for the next jump forward. "Get ready, you are about to grow." At the start of the pandemic, I felt lost. "This is as far as I can go. After all, I am in my 70s." Not true:

- When you think you've gone as far as you can, you've only just begun.

Well, okay, but maybe it's time to give up on this trumpet thing and do other things. I forgot the joy and wonder of life in tune. I picked up the horn and remembered:

- When you've lost momentum, go back to the basics.

Hopefully next time it won't take a virus shutting us down that gets us to think through these things. Practicing all these things in our daily lives will keep us ready, no matter what.

Rochester, MN
March, 2021

For Further Reading

- Art of Jazz Trumpet, The. John McNeil. (1999, Gerard & Sarzin).
- Deep Listening: A Composer's Sound Practice. Pauline Oliveros. (2005, iUniverse).
- Effortless Mastery: Liberating the Master Musician Within. Kenny Werner. (1996, Aebersold).
- Essential Elements for Jazz Ensemble. Mike Steinel. (2000, Hal Leonard).
- Failing Forward: Turning Mistakes into Stepping Stones for Success. John C. Maxwell. (2000, Nelson).
- Grit: The Power of Passion and Perseverance. Angela Duckworth. (2016, Scribner).
- History of Jazz, The. Ted Gioia. (1997, Oxford).
- How to Listen to Jazz. Ted Gioia. (2016, Basic Books).
- Improvisation for the Spirit: Live a More Creative, Spontaneous, and Courageous Life Using the Tools of Improv Comedy. Katie Goodman. (2006, Sourcebook).
- Improvising Jazz. Jerry Coker. (1964, Simon & Schuster).
- In Tune: Music as the Bridge to Mindfulness. Richard Wolf (2019, The Experiment).

- Inner Game of Music, The. Barry Green, W. Timothy Gallwey. (1986, Doubleday).
- Inner Game of Tennis, The: The Classic Guide to the Mental Side of Peak Performance. W. Timothy Gallwey. (1974, Random House).
- Insider's Guide to Understanding and Listening to Jazz, An. Jonny King. (1997, Walker).
- Jazz Standards, The: A Guide to the Repertoire. Ted Gioia. (2012, Oxford).
- Jazz: A History of America's Music (Companion volume to the PBS series). Geoffrey Ward and Ken Burns. (2000, Knopf).
- Kind of Blue: The Making of the Miles Davis Masterpiece. Ashley Kahn. (2000, Da Capo).
- Love Supreme, A: The Story of John Coltrane's Signature Album. Ashley Kahn and Elvin Jones. (2003, Penguin).
- Mayo Clinic Guide to Stress-Free Living, The. Amit Sood. (2013, Da Capo).
- Miles: The Autobiography. Miles Davis and Quincy Troupe. (1982, Simon & Schuster).
- Moving to Higher Ground: How Jazz Can Change Your Life. Wynton Marsalis and Geoffrey Ward. (2008, Random House).
- Music Lesson, The: A Spiritual Search for Growth Through Music. Victor L. Wooten. (2008, Penguin).
- Music: Ways of Listening. Elliott Schwartz. (1982, Bow Historical Books).
- Peak: Secrets from the New Science of Expertise. Anders Ericsson, Robert Pool. (2016, Houghton Mifflin).
- Pops: A Life of Louis Armstrong. Terry Teachout. (2009, Houghton Mifflin).
- Practicing: A Musician's Return to Music. Glenn Kurtz. Knopf. (2008, Doubleday).
- Psycho-Cybernetics: Updated and Expanded. Maxwell Maltz. (2015, Penguin).
- Seven Habits of Highly Successful People, The: Powerful Lessons in Personal Change. Stephen Covey. (1989, Free Press).

- Spirit of Music, The. Victor L. Wooten. (2021, Vintage).
- Spirit Seeker: John Coltrane's Musical Journey. Gary Golio and Rudy Gutierrez. (2012, Houghton Mifflin Harcourt).
- Spirits Rejoice!: Jazz and American Religion. Jason C. Bivins. (2015, Oxford).
- Study of Orchestration, The. Samuel Adler. (1989, 1982, Norton).
- This Is Your Brain on Music: The Science of a Human Obsession. Daniel J. Levitin. (2006, Penguin).
- Trumpet Voluntarily: A Holistic Guide to Maximizing Practice Through Efficiency. Paul Baron. (2016, Bugles Media).
- Waking the Spirit: A Musician's Journey Healing Body, Mind, and Soul. Andrew Schulman and Marvin A. McMillen. (2016, Picador).
- What Jazz Is. Jonny King. (1997, Walker).
- Wherever You Go, There You Are: Mindfulness Meditation in Everyday Life. Jon Kabat-Zinn. (1993, Hachette).
- Words Without Music: A Memoir. Philip Glass. (2015, Liveright).
- World in Six Songs: How the Musical Brain Created Human Nature, The. Daniel J. Levitin. (2008, Penguin).
- Zen in the Art of Archery. Eugen Herrigel (1948, 1953).

Acknowledgements

In addition to those mentioned at the beginning of the book, my thanks and deepest gratitude goes out to

- Birch Creek Performance Center and their Adult Band Camp in Egg Harbor, Wisconsin. (Chip Staley, Jim Stombres, and Steve Sveum). You weren't part of the first two years covered in the book, but you have given me another great outlet and boost. Looking forward to post-pandemic music. (https://birchcreek.org/)
- The team, coaches, and other students at Self-Publishing School. You are all amazing people. (https://self-publishingschool.com/friend/)
- The team and other students at Amazon Ads School helped me dig more deeply into what this book is all about. I was actually surprised. (https://selling-for-authors.teachable.com/p/amazon-ads-made-easy)
- Farley Sangels for permission to use the Ten Principles in chapters 1.21 and 1.22. Find him at https://lammastudios.com/.
- Betsy and Mike who encouraged me, and gave me a hard-time about my grandiosity and dreams. You keep me on my toes.
- Val. Without you I could never be who I have become. Your encouragement and support are beyond words.

About the Author

Barry Lehman has been playing trumpet since 1961, when, as an 8th grader he convinced his parents to allow him to join the Junior High Band. He continued playing while in college at Lehigh University in Bethlehem, PA. He is also a graduate of Moravian Theological Seminary and has a Doctor of Ministry degree in pastoral care and counseling from the Lutheran School of Theology, Chicago. Ordained in 1974, he served parishes of the Moravian Church in Pennsylvania, Wisconsin, and Minnesota. He retired from parish ministry in 2003. He has been a licensed alcohol and drug counselor since 1993 and a licensed professional counselor since 1999. He has worked as an addictions counselor in public schools and treatment centers. He retired in 2020 after twelve years from the Mayo Clinic in Rochester, MN. He decided to be a full-time author at that point. His book, *Christmas Grace and Light* contains stories he has written over the years for Christmas Eve. It is available on Amazon.

Since he attended the music camps in 2015, he has increased his music involvement and continues to play in a number of different groups including concert bands, big bands and a brass quintet. He has been a blogger since 2003 at Wanderings of a Post-Modern Pilgrim (http://pmpilgrim.blogspot.com/) and since 2015 at The Tuning Slide (http://www.tuningslide.net/). This book is the first two years of the Tuning Slide blog. He lives in Rochester, MN, with his wife,

Valerie, also a retired Moravian pastor. In addition to writing and music, he enjoys reading and photography. Further updates are at www.balehman.com.

The Shell Lake Faculty from 2015 and 2016 who have given me instruction, support and inspiration:

- Bob Baca, director of the Shell Lake Trumpet Workshop, is Professor of Trumpet and Director of Jazz Studies at the University of Wisconsin-Eau Claire. Bob is considered one of the top trumpet instructors and performers in the country.
- Bill Bergren is an educator and performer. He is the executive director of Synergy Jazz Foundation in Des Moines, IA.
- Matt Mealy holds degrees from the University of Wisconsin - Eau Claire and the Eastman School of Music in trumpet performance and music education. Currently, he teaches and performs in Western Wisconsin and the Twin Cities.
- Kyle Newmaster is a composer and performer. He holds a bachelor's degree in Music from the University of Wisconsin-Eau Claire and a master's degree in Composing for Contemporary Media from The Eastman School of Music in Rochester, New York.
- John Raymond, a performer and educator, is the assistant professor of music (jazz studies–trumpet) at The Indiana University Jacobs School of Music.
- Matt Stock, an active performer, is Fine Arts Librarian at the Oklahoma University School of Music.
- Paul Stodolka, performer and teacher, is a graduate of the University of Wisconsin- Eau Claire and the Manhattan School of Music in New York City.

Shell Lake Arts Center, located in Shell Lake, WI, provides a premium learning experience for all students in many areas of art, theater, and music. With its 50 years of programming, it is the longest-running program of its kind in the country and features experiences for youth and adults.

(https://www.shelllakeartscenter.org/)

NOW IT'S YOUR TURN

Self-Publishing
School

Discover the EXACT 3-step blueprint you need to become a bestselling author in as little as 3 months.

Self-Publishing School helped me, and now I want them to help you with this FREE resource to begin outlining your book!

Even if you're busy, bad at writing, or don't know where to start, you CAN write a bestseller and build your best life.

With tools and experience across a variety of niches and professions, Self-Publishing School is the only resource you need to take your book to the finish line!

DON'T WAIT

Say "YES" to becoming a bestseller:

https://self-publishingschool.com/friend/

Follow the steps on the page to get a FREE resource to get started on your book and unlock a discount to get started with Self-Publishing School.

Thank You for Reading
My Book!

I really appreciate all of your feedback, and I love hearing what you have to say. Please leave me an honest review on Amazon letting me know what you thought of the book. Thanks so much!

The complete 5½ years of the Tuning Slide Blog can be found at

www.tuningslide.net/blog

To see where I am going next, go to

https://www.subscribepage.com/aboutjazz

where you can sign-up for my email list and get a PDF of a special section from the blog on jazz.

Made in the USA
Monee, IL
12 September 2023